in Thai Red Curry

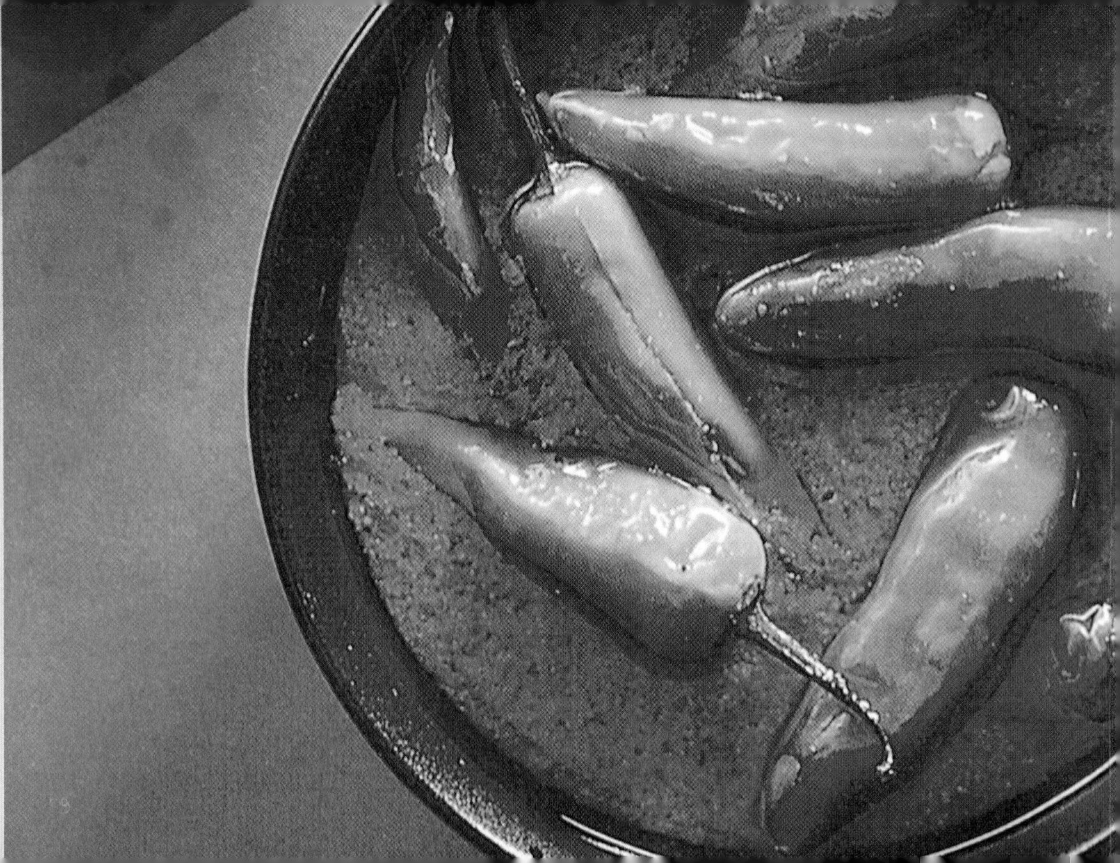

Mirchi Ka Salan

SANJEEV KAPOOR'S
SIMPLY VEGETARIAN
Recipes for the Indian Kitchen

Main Course III

SANJEEV KAPOOR'S
SIMPLY VEGETARIAN
Recipes for the Indian Kitchen

Main Course III

In association with Alyona Kapoor

PopulaR
prakashan

POPULAR PRAKASHAN PVT. LTD.

© 2004 by Sanjeev Kapoor

First Published 2004

(3887)

ISBN - 81-7991-139-X

PRINTED IN INDIA
By Thomson Press (I) Ltd.
18/35 Milestone, Delhi Mathura Road, Faridabad (Haryana)
and Published by Ramdas Bhatkal
for Popular Prakashan Pvt. Ltd.

Exclusively Distributed by : Impulse Marketing

Dedication

To all the lovers of authentic
food whose enthusiasm makes us
dig deeper into the
Khazana of Khana, and come up
with what is best
and most precious in cuisine.

Acknowledgements

A.I. Kazi
Afsheen Panjwani
Anand Bhandiwad
Mrs. Lata Lohana & Capt. K. K. Lohana
Debashish Mukherjee
Dhiraj Bolur
Drs. Meena & Ram Prabhoo
Ganesh Pednekar
Harpal Singh Sokhi
Jijesh Gangadharan
Jyotsna & Mayur Dvivedi
Kishore Roy
Mallika Shetty
Manish Anand
Namita Pusalkar
Namrata & Sanjiv Bahl

Neelima Acharya
Neena Murdeshwar
Pallavi Sharma
Pooja & Rajeev Kapoor
Priti Surve
Rajeev Matta
Rutika Samtani
Sanjay Bakshi
Satish Parab
Shivani Ganesh
Smeeta Bhatkal
Swapna Shinde
Tripta Bhagattjee
Vinayak Gawande

Note to the Readers

The only essential ingredient needed for adding passion to your life is the love for food! In a food lover's world recipes are the major ingredients for a successful life. Well, now success awaits you for what you are holding now is a goldmine of recipes! This book is the third of the series on vegetarian main courses. My main aim is not only to popularize Indian food globally but while doing so I am also propagating the fun in cooking at home. *Ghar ka khana* is dear to every Indian heart and whatever be your pinnacle of success in life, one nourishing and delicious meal at home, cooked by someone who loves you, is as essential to your spirit's well being as salt is to good food.

I strongly believe that with precise instructions, one who is fond of cooking irrespective of class, creed, age or colour can definitely bring on some good food to your table. This collection of recipes caters to those who not only are always looking out for different everyday dishes but also to those who love to make exotic dishes. It also caters to those who love to try out non-Indian food. Be it a colourful *Santung Garden Vegetable* or a wholesome *Middle Eastern Vegetable Stew* the taste of the end product is genuine as the recipe is precisely tested and tried. If the mood is adventurous do try out the *Korean Pickled Vegetables*. This dish never fails to surprise family and friends because it is attractive and very simply put together.

I can identify with those who can cook with passion and I can also identify with those who let fear overcome their dreams. I would say if one has to move ahead then dreams have to be bigger than fears. This is where my efforts by way of recipe books to help you understand that you can cook and with great success. Try out my favourite presentation called *Shaam Savera*. It is dear to my heart as it displays our patriotic colours. Other colourful and attractive dishes are to be seen under headings *Diwani Handi* and *Orange Broccoli*. Serve them as the main part of the meal with appropriate accompaniments.

It has always been my endeavour to regale you with dishes with a difference. Get out of the rut and enjoy *Masaledaar Tofu Bhurji, Mangodi Paanch Phoron* and something as humble as *tindli* gets a super treatment in *Tindli Moongphali.*

All recipes serve four and form part of a menu. Cook with confidence, style and with a smile!

CONTENTS

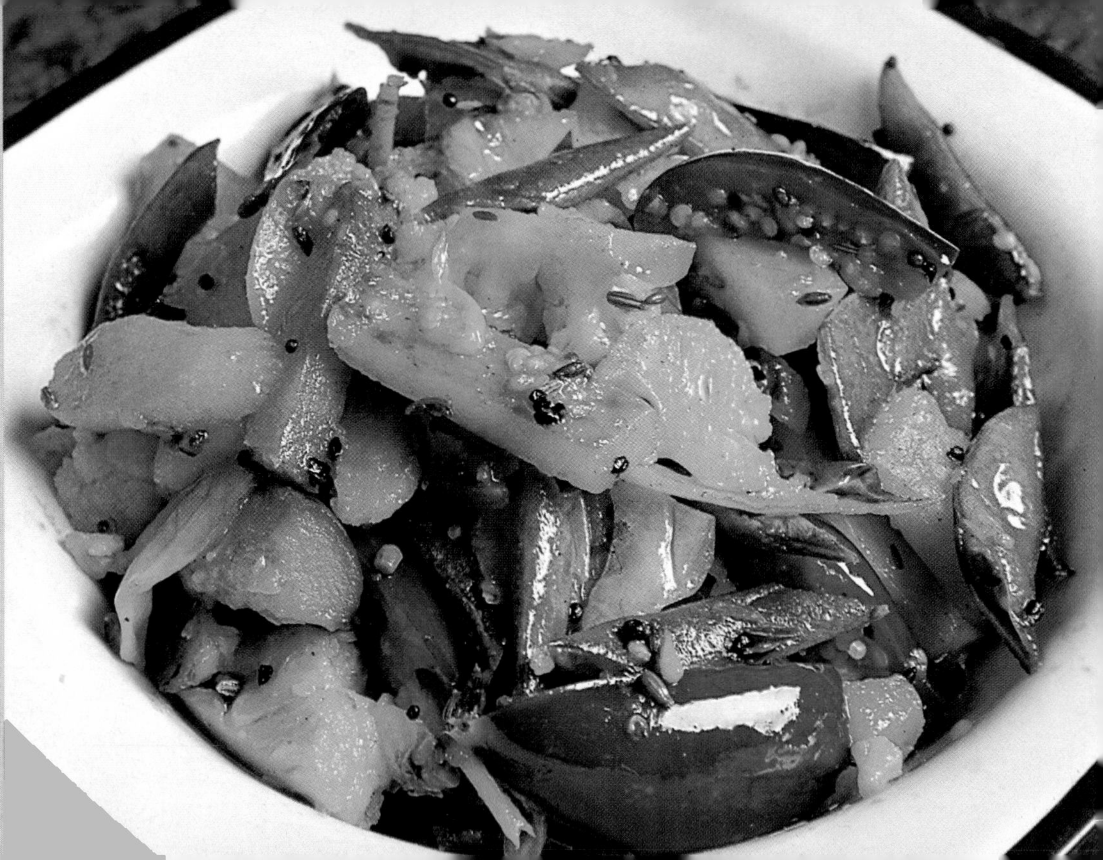

Labra

LABRA

INGREDIENTS

French beans 10
Broad beans *(papri/sem)* 10
Potatoes .... 1 large sized
Sweet potatoes 2
White radishes... 2 medium sized
Red pumpkin................. 100 gms
Cabbage .... ½ small sized
Green chillies 2
Cauliflower .... ½ medium sized

Round brinjals......... 2 small sized
Ginger .... 1 inch piece
Mustard oil .... 1 tbsp
Paanch phoron .... ½ tsp
Red chillies whole 3
Turmeric powder .... 1 tsp
Salt .... to taste
Sugar .... ¾ tsp

METHOD OF PREPARATION

1   String French beans and *papri*. Wash and cut each into two. Peel
    potatoes, sweet potatoes, white radishes and red pumpkin. Wash
    and cut all the vegetables into slices. Place potatoes and sweet
    potatoes in water to avoid discolouring. Wash, remove core and

shred cabbage. Remove stems, wash and slit green chillies. Wash cauliflower and break into small florets. Remove stems, wash and cut brinjals into four pieces. Keep in water to avoid discolouring. Peel, wash and grind ginger to a paste.

2 Heat oil, add *paanch phoron* and whole red chillies. When they change colour, add all the vegetables and stir.

3 Add turmeric powder and ginger paste and mix well. Cover and cook on low heat till vegetables are cooked.

4 Increase heat so that all the moisture dries up. Add salt, sugar, slit green chillies and mix well. Cook for two minutes and remove pan from heat.

5 Serve hot.

CHEF'S TIP

Paanch phoron is a mixture of equal amounts of mustard seeds *(rai)*, fenugreek seeds *(methi)*, onion seeds *(kalonji)*, fennel seeds *(saunf)* and cumin seeds *(jeera)*.

SHAAM SAVERA

INGREDIENTS

For kofta
Spinach .... 2 medium bundles
Green chillies 2
Garlic .... 6-8 cloves
Cornstarch .... 3 tbsps
Salt .... to taste
Cottage cheese (*paneer*) .... 125 gms
Oil.............................. to deep fry
For tomato gravy
Ginger .... 1 inch piece
Garlic .... 5-6 cloves
Green chillies 2
Tomato puree .... 2 cups
Butter .... 3 tbsps
Cloves 6
Green cardamoms 4
Bay leaf 1
Red chilli powder .... 1 tbsp
Garam masala powder .... ½ tsp
Salt .... to taste
Sugar/honey .... 3 tbsps
Dry fenugreek leaves (*kasuri methi*)
.... ½ tsp
Fresh cream .... 1 cup

METHOD OF PREPARATION

1   Clean, trim and wash spinach in plenty of running water. Blanch in
    boiling hot water for two to three minutes and refresh in cold water.
    Squeeze out water and chop finely.

2   Remove stems, wash and finely chop green chillies. Peel, wash and finely chop garlic.

3   Mix the spinach, green chillies, garlic, cornstarch and salt to taste well. Divide into twelve equal portions.

4   Grate cottage cheese. Add salt to taste and mash well. Divide into twelve equal balls.

5   Take spinach portions, flatten it on your palm and stuff cottage cheese balls in it. Shape into a ball.

6   Heat sufficient oil in a *kadai* and deep-fry balls in moderately hot oil for five minutes. Drain and keep aside.

7   To make tomato gravy peel, wash and grind ginger and garlic to a fine paste. Remove stems, wash and finely chop green chillies.

8   Heat butter in a pan, add cloves, green cardamoms and bay leaf. When they crackle, add ginger-garlic paste and green chillies. Cook for two minutes.

9   Add tomato puree, red chilli powder, *garam masala* powder, salt and one cup of water. Bring it to a boil, reduce heat and simmer for ten minutes. Add sugar or honey. Crush *kasuri methi* and add it to the gravy. Stir in fresh cream.

10 Serve *koftas*, halved and placed on a bed of tomato gravy. Do not boil *koftas* in the gravy as they may break.

CHEF'S TIP

Before proceeding with all the *koftas*, deep fry one and check if they are breaking. If they break, add some more cornstarch in spinach mixture and then deep fry in hot oil.

PANEER JALFRAEZI

INGREDIENTS

Cottage cheese (*paneer*) ... 400 gms	Red chillies whole 2
Tomatoes .... 2 medium sized	Oil .... 3 tbsps
Capsicums.......... 2 medium sized	Cumin seeds .... 1 tsp
Onions................ 2 medium sized	Red chilli powder .... 1½ tsps
Ginger .... 2 inch piece	Turmeric powder .... ½ tsp
Green chillies 1–2	Salt .... to taste
Fresh coriander leaves	Vinegar .... 1½ tbsps
.... ¼ medium bunch	*Garam masala* powder .... 1 tsp

METHOD OF PREPARATION

1 Cut *paneer* into two inch long pieces. Wash and cut tomatoes and capsicums into half, deseed and cut them into two inch long slices with one-fourth inch width. Peel, wash onions and cut into thick slices. Separate the different layers of onions.

2 Peel, wash and cut ginger into julienne. Remove stems, wash and

chop green chillies. Clean, wash and finely chop coriander leaves. Remove stems and break red chillies into two pieces.

3   Heat oil in a *kadai*. Add cumin seeds. When they change colour add red chillies. Add ginger julienne and sliced onions. Sauté for half a minute.

4   Add red chilli powder and turmeric powder. Stir well and add capsicum. Cook for two to three minutes. Add *paneer* fingers and toss. Add salt and vinegar and cook for two to three minutes. Stir in tomato pieces and *garam masala* powder.

5   Serve hot garnished with chopped coriander leaves.

SANTUNG GARDEN VEGETABLES

INGREDIENTS

Baby carrots	3-4	Oil	2 tbsps
Zucchini	4 medium sized	Star anise	1
Celery	2 stalks	Five spice powder	1 tsp
Leeks	2	Lemon juice	2 tbsps
Baby corns	6-8	Honey	1 tbsp
Snow peas or flat beans	8-10	Salt	to taste
Pineapple	2 slices	Pepper powder	¼ tsp
Tofu	100 gms	Lemon rind	½ tsp
Cornstarch	1 tbsp		

METHOD OF PREPARATION

1 Peel, wash and cut baby carrots into half lengthwise. Wash and cut zucchini into thin roundels.

27

2   Wash, trim and slice celery and leeks. Wash celery leaves and keep aside for garnish.

3   Wash and cut baby corns into half lengthwise. String, wash and halve snow peas or flat beans. Cut tofu and pineapple slices into one inch sized pieces. Dissolve cornstarch in a quarter cup of water.

4   Heat oil in a wok. Add star anise, baby carrots, celery, leeks, snow peas and baby corn. Stir-fry for about three to four minutes on high heat. Add five-spice powder. Stir. Add zucchini and stir.

5   Add tofu and pineapple, stir gently.

6   Add half a cup of hot water and bring to a boil. Stir in blended cornstarch and cook for half a minute on high heat, stirring continuously.

7   Stir in lemon juice and honey. Add salt and pepper powder.

8   Serve hot garnished with lemon rind and celery leaves.

CHEF'S TIP

Five spice powder can be made at home by grinding together equal quantities of star anise, cinnamon, fennel seeds, cloves and Sichuan pepper.

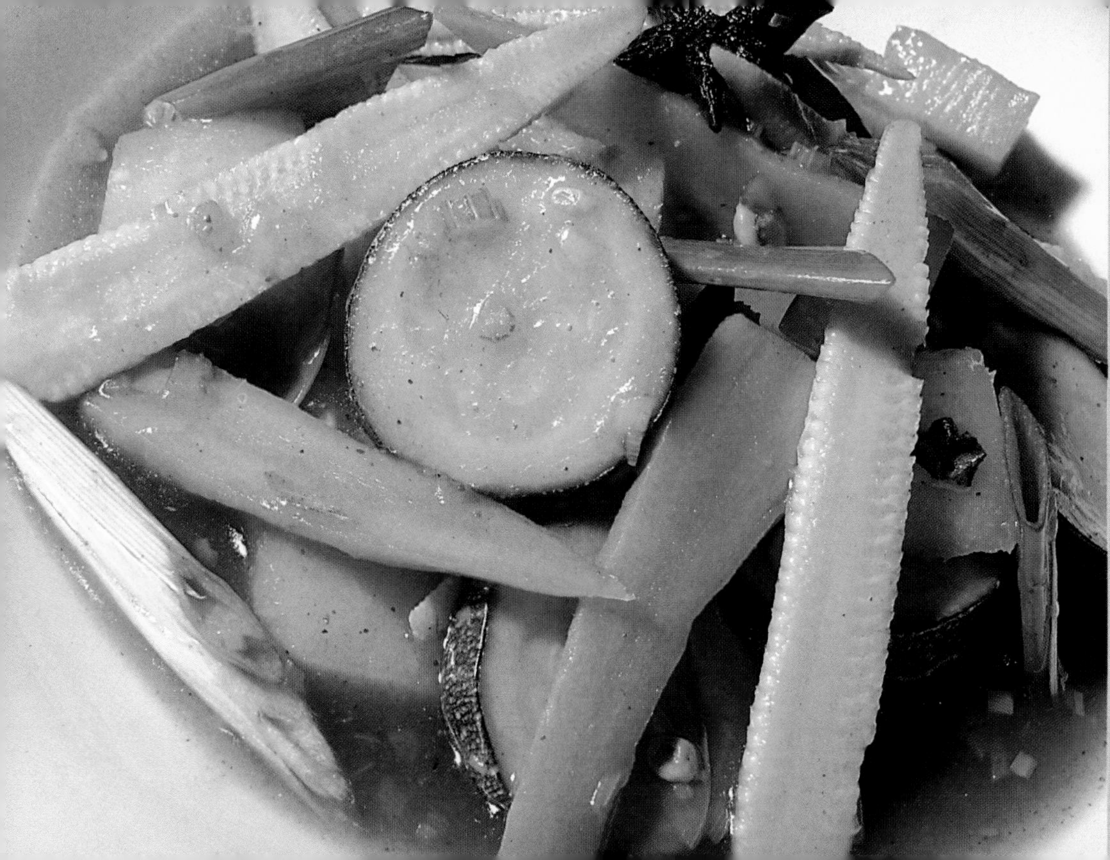

Santung Garden Vegetables

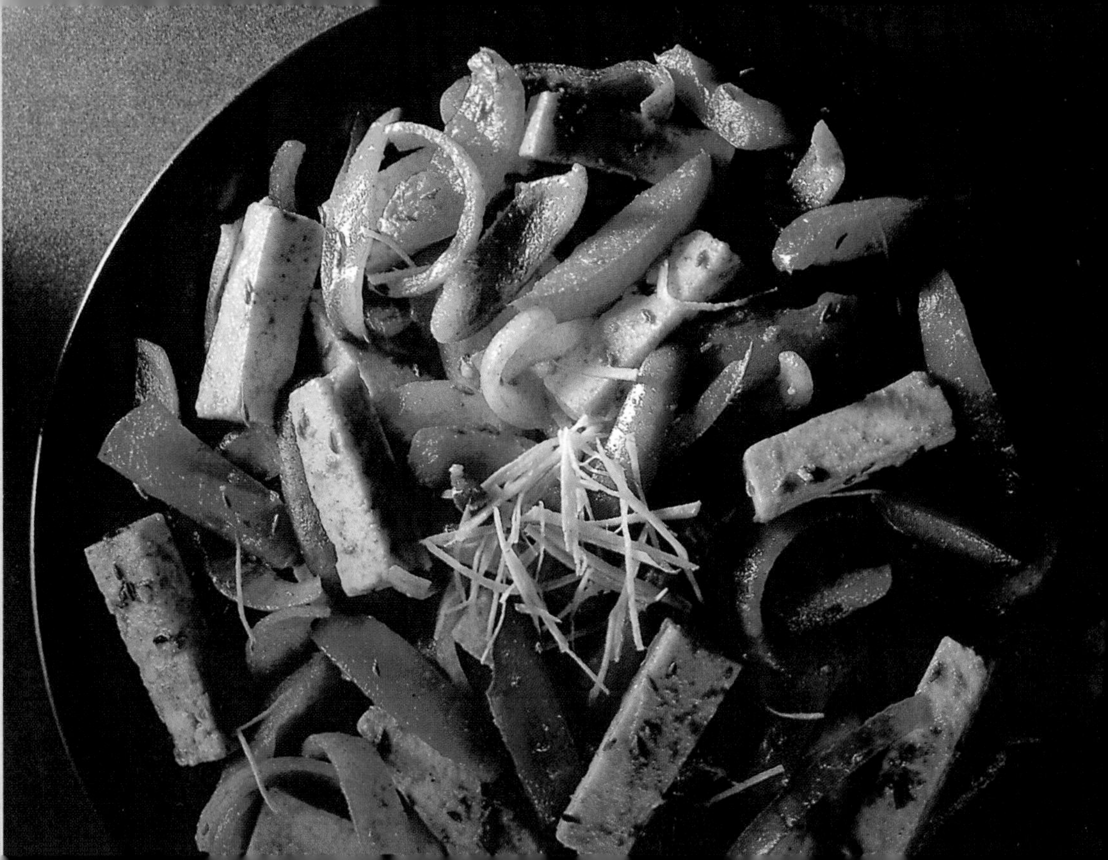

Paneer Jhalfraizee

Rosemary Potatoes

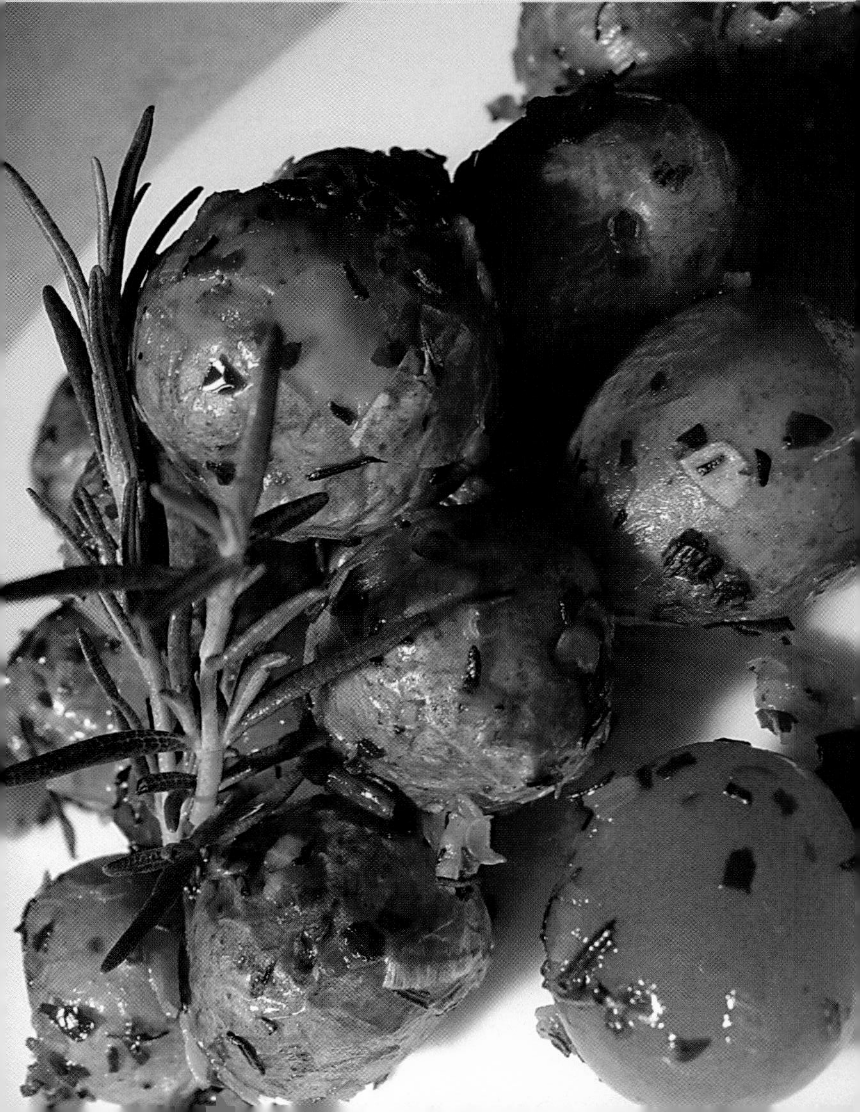

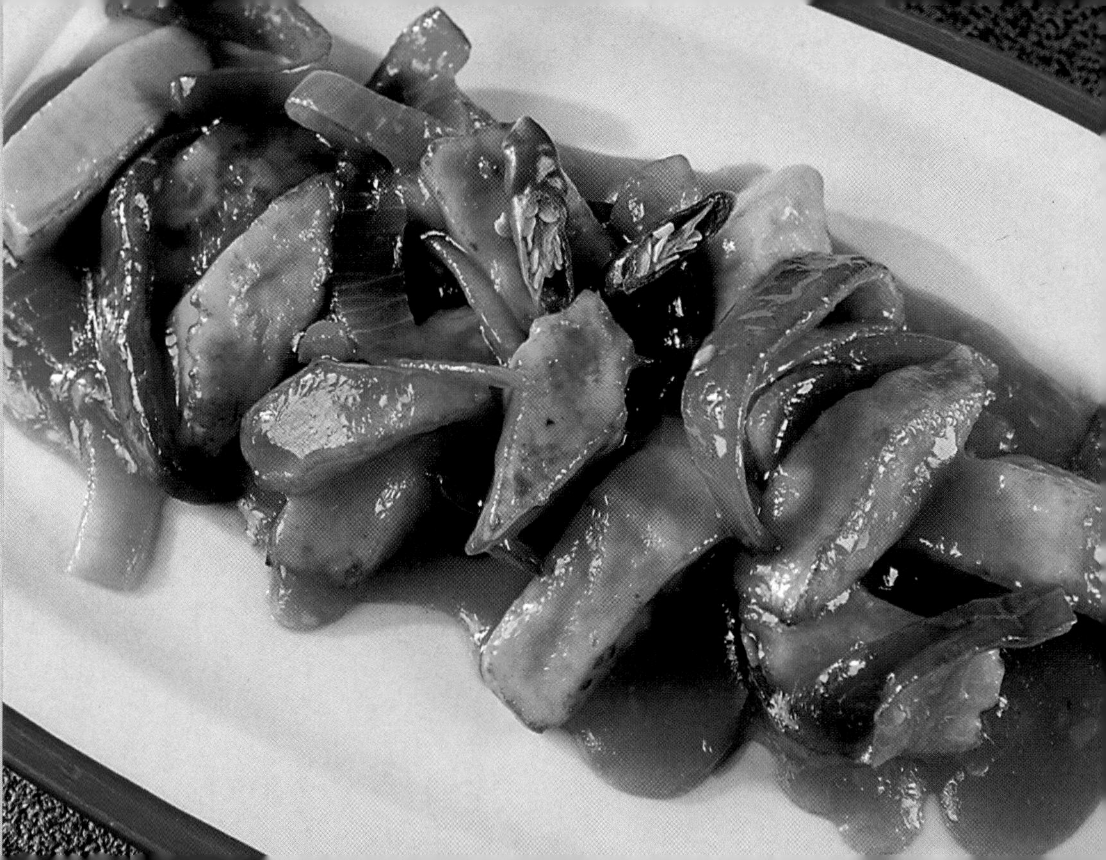

Chilli Paneer

CHILLI
PANEER

INGREDIENTS

Cottage cheese (*paneer*) ... 200 gms
Cornstarch .... 4 tbsps
Oil.............. 2 tbsps + to deep fry
Onions...................................... 2
Garlic .... 3-4 cloves
Green chillies 3-4
Capsicum .... 1 large sized

Vegetable stock .... ½ cup
Salt .... to taste
White pepper powder .... ½ tsp
Soy sauce .... 2 tbsps
Chilli sauce......................... 1 tbsp
Ajinomoto .... ¼ tsp

METHOD OF PREPARATION

1   Cut *paneer* into diamond shaped medium sized pieces. Heat sufficient
    oil in a wok, roll *paneer* pieces in cornstarch and deep fry on medium
    heat until the edges start to turn brown. Drain onto an absorbent
    paper and keep aside.

2   Blend remaining cornstarch (nearly one tablespoon) in a quarter cup of water and keep aside.
3   Peel, wash onions and cut into thick slices. Peel, wash and crush garlic. Remove stems, wash and slice green chillies. Wash, halve, deseed and cut capsicum into thick strips.
4   Heat two tablespoons of oil in a wok, add garlic and stir-fry for a minute. Add green chillies, onions and capsicum. Sauté for two to three minutes.
5   Add fried *paneer* and stir in vegetable stock. Add salt, white pepper powder, soy sauce, chilli sauce, Ajinomoto and stir well.
6   Stir in blended cornstarch and cook on high heat, stirring and tossing till sauce thickens to coat the *paneer* and the vegetables. Serve immediately.

ROSEMARY POTATOES

INGREDIENTS

Baby potatoes	16-20	Olive oil	2 tbsps
Spring onions	2	Salt	to taste
Cherry tomatoes	12-15	Paprika	1 tsp
Fresh/dry rosemary	1 tsp	Brown sugar	1 tsp

METHOD OF PREPARATION

1   Scrub and wash potatoes very well to remove any soil. Boil or roast them till three-fourth done.

2   Wash, trim and finely chop spring onions with the greens. Reserve greens for garnish. Wash cherry tomatoes. Wash and chop rosemary if using the fresh one.

3   Heat oil in a non-stick pan and add parboiled potatoes. Cook on high heat, tossing continuously till potatoes turn crisp and a little golden brown. Sprinkle chopped rosemary and spring onions. Mix well. Reduce heat and cook for another five minutes.

4   When potatoes are fully done, add cherry tomatoes. Season with salt, paprika and brown sugar.

5   Serve hot garnished with spring onion greens.

VEGETABLES IN THAI RED CURRY

INGREDIENTS

Carrots .... 4 medium sized
Capsicum .... 1 medium sized
Cauliflower .... ½ small sized
Cabbage .... ½ small sized
French beans 10-12
Roasted peanuts .... 4 tbsps
Oil.. 1 tbsp
Lemon juice .... 1 tsp
Salt .... to taste
Thin coconut milk .... ¾ cup

Bean sprouts .... 1 cup
For Red curry paste
Red chillies whole 8
Lemon grass .... 4 inch stalk
Onions .... 2 medium sized
Garlic .... 4 cloves
Coriander seeds .... 4 tsps
Cumin seeds .... 2 tsps
Peppercorns 6
Salt .... to taste

METHOD OF PREPARATION

1   Peel, wash carrots and cut into three-centimetre long sticks.
2   Wash capsicum, halve, deseed and cut into three-centimetre long pieces.

3   Wash and cut cauliflower into small florets. Wash, remove core and cut cabbage into one-centimetre sized pieces. String, wash French beans and cut them into three-centimetre long pieces. Crush roasted peanuts coarsely.

4   To make red curry paste, remove stems of red chillies. Wash lemon grass. Peel, wash and chop onions and garlic. Mix red chillies, lemon grass, onions, garlic, coriander seeds, cumin seeds, peppercorns, salt and a little water. Grind into a fine paste.

5   Heat oil in a non-stick pan, add carrots, cauliflower, French beans and half a cup of water. Cook on medium heat for five to six minutes, stirring occasionally. Add cabbage and capsicum. Mix well. Add red curry paste, stir well, cook on high heat for one or two minutes.

6   Stir in lemon juice and salt. Mix well and add thin coconut milk. Simmer for two minutes and stir in bean sprouts and crushed roasted peanuts. Serve hot.

MIRCHI KA SALAN

INGREDIENTS

Green chillies .... 18-20 large sized
Oil.............. 2 tbsps + to deep-fry
Onion .... 1 medium sized
Ginger .... 1 inch piece
Garlic .... 6-8 cloves
Curry leaves 8-10
Sesame seeds .... 2 tbsps
Coriander seeds................ 1 tbsp

Cumin seeds .... 1 tsp
Roasted peanuts (peeled) ... ½ cup
Red chillies whole 2
Mustard seeds....................... 1 tsp
Turmeric powder .... 1 tsp
Tamarind pulp.................. 2 tbsps
Salt .... to taste

METHOD OF PREPARATION

1   Wash, wipe and slit green chillies lengthwise without removing the stems. Heat sufficient oil in a *kadai* and deep fry chillies in hot oil for one minute. Drain onto an absorbent paper and keep aside.

2   Peel, wash and grate onion. Peel, wash ginger and garlic and chop roughly. Wash and pat dry curry leaves.

3   Dry roast sesame seeds, coriander seeds and cumin seeds. Make paste of roasted sesame seeds, coriander seeds, cumin seeds, roasted peanuts, whole red chillies, ginger and garlic.

4   Heat two tablespoons of oil in a pan, add mustard seeds, let it crackle and add curry leaves. Add onion and sauté, stirring continuously, till onion turns light golden brown.

5   Add turmeric powder and mix well. Add *masala* paste and cook for three minutes, stirring continuously. Stir in one and a half cups of water and bring to a boil. Reduce heat and cook for ten minutes. Add tamarind pulp dissolved in half a cup of water, if it is too thick.

6   Add fried green chillies and salt and cook on low heat for eight to ten minutes.

Note: In Hyderabad, *Mirchi Ka Salan* is traditionally served as an accompaniment to *biryanis*. Some people like to add grated coconut to the *masala* paste, but I prefer *Mirchi ka Salan* without coconut. This gravy is referred to as *Tili* (*Til* - Sesame) *aur Falli* (*Moongfalli* - Peanuts) gravy.

PALAK PANEER

INGREDIENTS

Spinach .... 2 large bunches
Cottage cheese (*paneer*) ... 200 gms
Green chillies 2-3
Garlic .... 8-10 cloves
Oil...................................... 3 tbsps

Cumin seeds .... ½ tsp
Salt .... to taste
Lemon juice .... 1 tbsp
Fresh cream .... 4 tbsps

METHOD OF PREPARATION

1   Remove stems, wash spinach thoroughly in running water. Blanch in salted boiling water for two minutes. Refresh in chilled water. Squeeze out excess water. Remove stems, wash and roughly chop green chillies.

2   Grind spinach into a fine paste along with green chillies.

3   Dice *paneer* into one inch by one inch by half inch pieces. Peel, wash and chop garlic.

4   Heat oil in a pan. Add cumin seeds. When they begin to change colour, add chopped garlic and sauté for half a minute. Add the spinach puree and stir. Check seasoning. Add water if required.

5   When the gravy comes to a boil, add the *paneer* and mix well. Stir in lemon juice. Finally add fresh cream.

6   Serve hot.

GAJAR DAL MEL

INGREDIENTS

Bengal gram spilt (*chana dal*) ... ¾ cup
Carrots .... 3-4 medium sized
Onions .... 2 medium sized
Ginger .... 1 inch piece
Garlic .... 4-5 cloves
Tomatoes .... 2 medium sized
Fresh coriander leaves ....
.... ¼ medium bunch

Oil .... 1½ tsps
Bay leaf 1
Cumin seeds .... 1 tsp
Red chilli powder .... 1 tsp
Coriander powder .... 1½ tsps
Turmeric powder .... ½ tsp
Salt .... to taste

METHOD OF PREPARATION

1   Pick, wash and soak *chana dal* for one to two hours in two cups of
    water.
2   Peel, wash and cut carrots into one centimeter sized cubes. Peel,
    wash and chop onions, ginger and garlic separately. Wash tomatoes
    and chop finely. Clean, wash and finely chop coriander leaves.

3   Heat oil in a non-stick pan, add bay leaf, cumin seeds and cook briefly. Add onions and cook over medium heat till onions turn translucent. Add ginger and garlic and stir-fry for half a minute.

4   Reduce heat and add red chilli powder, coriander powder, turmeric powder and stir to mix well. Add tomatoes and continue to cook for three to four minutes, stirring occasionally.

5   Drain and add soaked *chana dal* and carrot cubes and mix well. Add one cup of water and salt to taste.

6   Cook on high heat till water begins to boil, lower heat, cover and simmer till *dal* is well cooked and *masala* is almost dry. Adjust salt.

7   Garnish with chopped coriander leaves and serve hot.

MASALEDAAR TOFU BHURJI

INGREDIENTS

Tofu (beancurd) .... 300 gms
Onions .... 2 medium sized
Ginger .... 1 inch piece
Tomatoes .... 2 medium sized
Capsicums .... 2 medium sized
Green chillies 2
Fresh coriander leaves ....
.... ¼ medium bunch

Oil .... 1 ½ tsps
Cumin seeds .... 1 tsp
Turmeric powder .... ½ tsp
Cumin powder .... 1 tsp
Coriander powder .... 1 tbsp
Red chilli powder .... 1 tsp
Salt .... to taste

METHOD OF PREPARATION

1 Drain tofu and crumble it into small pieces.
2 Peel, wash and finely chop onions and ginger. Wash and finely chop tomatoes. Wash, halve, deseed and finely chop capsicums. Remove

stems, wash and finely chop green chillies. Clean, wash and finely chop coriander leaves.

3   Heat oil in a non-stick pan, add cumin seeds and cook till it starts to change colour. Add onions, ginger and green chillies. Stir-fry till onions become translucent.

4   Dissolve turmeric powder, cumin powder, coriander powder and red chilli powder in half a cup of water and add this to the pan. Cook on medium heat for half a minute, stirring continuously.

5   Add tomatoes and cook on high heat for two minutes, stirring continuously. Stir in tofu and capsicums and salt to taste. Mix well.

6   Reduce heat and cook for two to three minutes, tossing frequently to prevent sticking, which happens when cooking tofu.

7   Serve hot sprinkled with coriander leaves.

CEYLON KOOTU

INGREDIENTS

Green peas (shelled) .... ½ cup
Carrots .... 2 medium sized
Potato .... 1 medium sized
Knol kohl (gaanth gobhi) ....
.... 1 medium sized
French beans 8-10
Cauliflower .... 1 small sized
Pure ghee .... 2 tbsps
Cashewnuts 15

Onion .... 1 medium sized
Tomato .... 1 medium sized
Green chillies 6
Curry leaves 20
Coconut (scraped) .... 1½ cups
Coconut oil .... 4 tbsps
Mustard seeds .... ½ tsp
Salt .... to taste
Rice flour .... 1 tsp

METHOD OF PREPARATION

1 Wash and drain green peas. Peel and wash carrots, potato and knol
   khol. Cut into small dices. String, wash and chop French beans
   finely. Wash and break cauliflower into small florets and dice into
   small pieces. Parboil these vegetables in salted water. Drain and
   keep aside.

2 Heat *ghee* and fry cashewnuts to a light brown. Remove from heat and let cashewnuts soak in the *ghee*.

3 Peel, wash and chop onion. Wash and quarter tomato and keep aside. Remove stems, wash and slit green chillies. Wash curry leaves and pat dry.

4 Soak scraped coconut in two cups of warm water. Grind and squeeze out a thick milk. Grind residue with one cup of water to get a second extract.

5 Heat coconut oil and temper with mustard seeds and curry leaves. Add onion, green chillies and sauté till onion turns translucent. Add tomato and stir over high heat and cook for two to three minutes.

6 Add parboiled vegetables and toss well. Blend rice flour in the second extract of coconut and pour into the *kootu*, add salt and simmer till it thickens.

7 Remove from heat, add the first extract and bring back to simmering point.

8 Stir in fried cashewnuts along with *ghee* and serve hot.

CHEF'S TIP

Squeeze in a lemon after removing from heat to enhance the flavour of the *kootu*.

MANGODI PAANCH PHORAN

INGREDIENTS

Green gram dumplings, dried.....
(*mangodi*) .... 1 cup
Skimmed milk yogurt........ 1 cup
Gram flour (*besan*) .... 1 tbsp
Turmeric powder................. ½ tsp
Red chilli powder............ 1½ tsps
Coriander powder............. 1 tbsp
Fresh coriander leaves...............
........................¼ medium bunch

Oil .... 1½ tsps
Asafoetida .... a pinch
Mustard seeds..................... ¼ tsp
Cumin seeds....................... ¼ tsp
Fennel seeds (*saunf*) .... ¼ tsp
Fenugreek seeds................. ¼ tsp
Onion seeds (*kalonji*) .... ¼ tsp
Salt .... to taste

METHOD OF PREPARATION

1   Whisk yogurt with *besan*, turmeric powder, red chilli powder,
    coriander powder and one cup of water. Ensure that there are no
    lumps. Clean, wash and chop coriander leaves.

2   Heat a non-stick frying pan and dry roast the *mangodi*, stirring continuously till they turn golden brown. Remove and keep aside.
3   Heat oil in a pan. Add mustard seeds and asafoetida, cumin seeds, fennel seeds, fenugreek seeds and onion seeds. When they begin to crackle, reduce heat and add yogurt mixture and salt to taste.
4   Stir well and bring it to a boil. Add *mangodi* and chopped coriander leaves.
5   Reduce heat and simmer till *mangodi* are soft and cooked. This requires approximately eight to ten minutes. However this time can change depending on the quality and size of *mangodi* that you use.

Note: Readymade sun-dried *mangodi* are readily available at grocery stores.

Mangodi Paanch Phoran

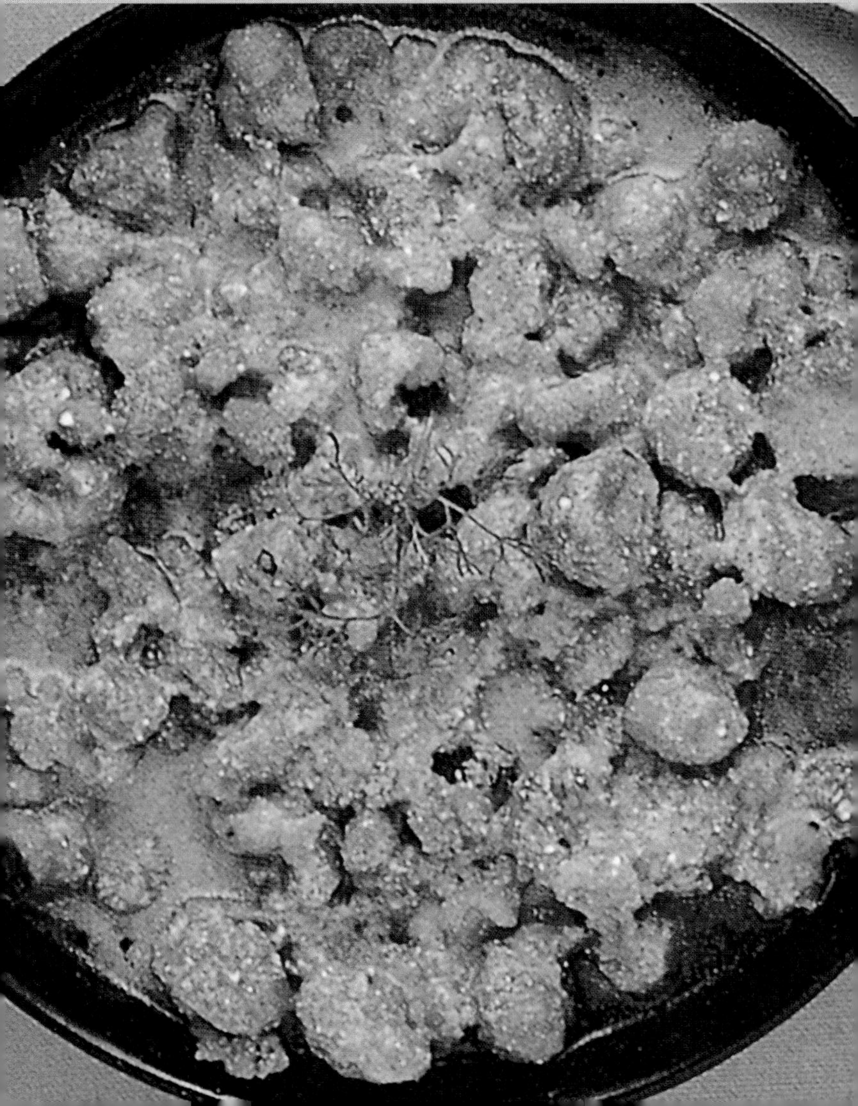

Dahi Bhindi

DAHI BHINDI

INGREDIENTS

Tender lady fingers (*bhindi*) .... 400 gms
Green chillies 3-4
Ginger .... 1 inch piece
Peppercorns 4-5
Skimmed milk yogurt .... 1½ cups
Red chillies whole 2

Gram flour (*besan*) .... 1 tbsp
Oil .... 1½ tsps
Cumin seeds .... 1 tsp
Coriander powder .... 1 tbsp
Turmeric powder .... ½ tsp
Salt .... to taste

METHOD OF PREPARATION

1   Wash and wipe dry lady fingers with a clean and absorbent kitchen towel.
2   Trim heads and tails. Remove stems, wash and slit green chillies.
3   Peel, wash and grind ginger with peppercorns to a fine paste.

4   Whisk skimmed milk yogurt. Remove stems and break red chillies into two.

5   Dry roast *besan* in a non-stick pan on low heat, stirring continuously till it gives a roasted aroma. Keep aside to cool.

6   Heat oil in a non-stick pan, add red chillies, cumin seeds and stir-fry briefly.

7   Add green chillies, coriander powder, turmeric powder, *besan* and stir well.

8   Add trimmed lady fingers, salt to taste and cook over medium heat, stirring frequently for five minutes.

9   Stir in ginger-peppercorn paste. Reduce heat and add whisked yogurt, mix well and cook covered for eight to ten minutes, stirring occasionally or till lady fingers are completely cooked.

BEANS PARUPPU USLI

INGREDIENTS

French beans .... 250 gms
Green chillies 2
Red chillies whole 2
Curry leaves 8-10
Sesame oil .... 4-5 tbsps
Mustard seeds ....½ tsp
Black gram split (*dhuli urad dal*).
.... 1 tsp
Salt .... to taste
Dal paste
Bengal gram split (*chana dal*) ... ¼ cup

Black gram split (*dhuli urad dal*)
.... 2 tbsps
Green gram split (*dhuli moong dal*)
.... 2 tbsps
Pigeon pea split (*toovar dal*) .....
....¼ cup
Red chillies whole 6
Asafoetida .... ¼ tsp

METHOD OF PREPARATION

1   String, wash and cut French beans into half centimeter sized pieces.
    Cook beans in salted boiling water for two to three minutes. Drain
    well and reserve. Remove stems, wash and finely chop green chillies.
    Remove stems and break red chillies into two. Wash and pat dry
    curry leaves.

2   For the paste, wash and soak all the *dals* for about twenty minutes in double the quantity of water. Remove stems and break red chillies into two. Drain *dals* and grind to a thick paste with red chillies, asafoetida and salt to taste. Add water if required.

3   Apply a little oil on a piece of banana leaf according to the size of the steamer or the pressure cooker. Spread *dal* paste evenly on it and steam in a cooker for fifteen minutes or till cooked. Insert a toothpick or needle into the *dal* mixture and if it comes out clean then it is cooked.

4   Turn out cooked *dal* on a large plate and cool. Crumble cooked *dal* to a coarse powder with your palm and fingers. If *dal* is quite dry and solid, then you can blend it briefly in a food processor to crumble.

5   Heat oil in a shallow pan, temper with mustard seeds, broken red chillies, *urad dal* and curry leaves.

6   Stir-fry briefly and add chopped green chillies.

7   Add the cooked beans and crumbled *dal* mixture. Toss on high heat for two to three minutes. Reduce heat and cook, stirring frequently for five to six minutes or till the beans and *dal* start sizzling.

8   Adjust seasoning and serve hot.

MATAR NARALACHI USSAL

INGREDIENTS

Green peas (shelled) ..... 1¼ cups
Green chillies 4
Ginger .... 1 inch piece
Fresh coriander leaves . ¼ small bunch
Curry leaves 5-6
Coconut (scraped) .... 1 cup

Oil .... 4 tbsps
Mustard seeds .... ½ tsp
Turmeric powder .... ¼ tsp
Cumin powder .... 1 tsp
Salt .... to taste
Lemon juice .... ½ tbsp

METHOD OF PREPARATION

1 Wash and drain green peas. Remove stems, wash and finely chop green chillies. Peel, wash and finely chop ginger. Clean, wash and finely chop coriander leaves. Wash and pat dry curry leaves.
2 Grind half of the scraped coconut with half a cup of water. Extract coconut milk. Heat oil in a pan. Add mustard seeds and let them crackle. Add curry leaves.
3 Add green chillies and ginger. Cook for a few seconds. Add green peas and remaining scraped coconut. Mix it well. Cook on low heat.
4 Add turmeric powder, cumin powder, salt, lemon juice and a quarter cup of water. Mix well.
5 Cover and cook till green peas are done. Stir in coconut milk.
6 Serve hot, garnished with chopped coriander leaves.

PALAK
BAHAR

INGREDIENTS

Spinach .... 2 medium bunches
Green chillies 3
Carrots .... 2 medium sized
French beans 5-6
Cauliflower .... ¼ medium sized
Onion .... 1 large sized
Tomatoes .... 2 medium sized
Ginger .... 1 inch piece
Garlic .... 4 cloves

Fresh coriander leaves .... a few sprigs
Oil .... 1½ tbsps
Nutmeg powder .... ¼ tsp
Salt .... to taste
Cumin seeds .... ½ tsp
Lemon juice .... 1 tsp
Red chilli powder .... 1 ½ tsps
Garam masala powder .... 2 tsps

METHOD OF PREPARATION

1   Clean and trim spinach and wash in running water several times.
    Blanch it in boiling hot water for two to three minutes. Drain excess
    water and refresh spinach leaves in cold water. Remove stems, wash

and chop green chillies. Puree spinach in a blender along with one green chilli.

2   Peel, wash and cut carrots into thin diagonal slices. String, wash French beans and cut into diamond shaped pieces. Wash and separate cauliflower into small florets. Blanch these vegetables in boiling water for two to three minutes. Drain.

3   Peel, wash and chop onion. Wash and chop tomatoes. Peel, wash and chop ginger and garlic. Clean, wash and chop coriander leaves.

4   Heat half of the oil, add ginger and garlic, stir-fry.

5   Add onion and remaining green chillies. Stir-fry till onions are pinkish in colour. Add nutmeg powder and continue cooking on medium heat for a couple of minutes, stirring frequently.

6   Add pureed spinach, cook it for a minute and add salt. Keep it aside.

7   Heat the remaining oil in a frying pan, add cumin seeds and when it starts to change colour, add tomatoes. Cook on a medium heat for three to four minutes, stirring continuously. Add blanched vegetables and stir-fry lightly.

8   Add lemon juice and season with salt and red chilli powder. Add *garam masala* powder and chopped coriander leaves.
9   Spread prepared spinach on a flat serving dish and place cooked vegetables in the center and serve hot.

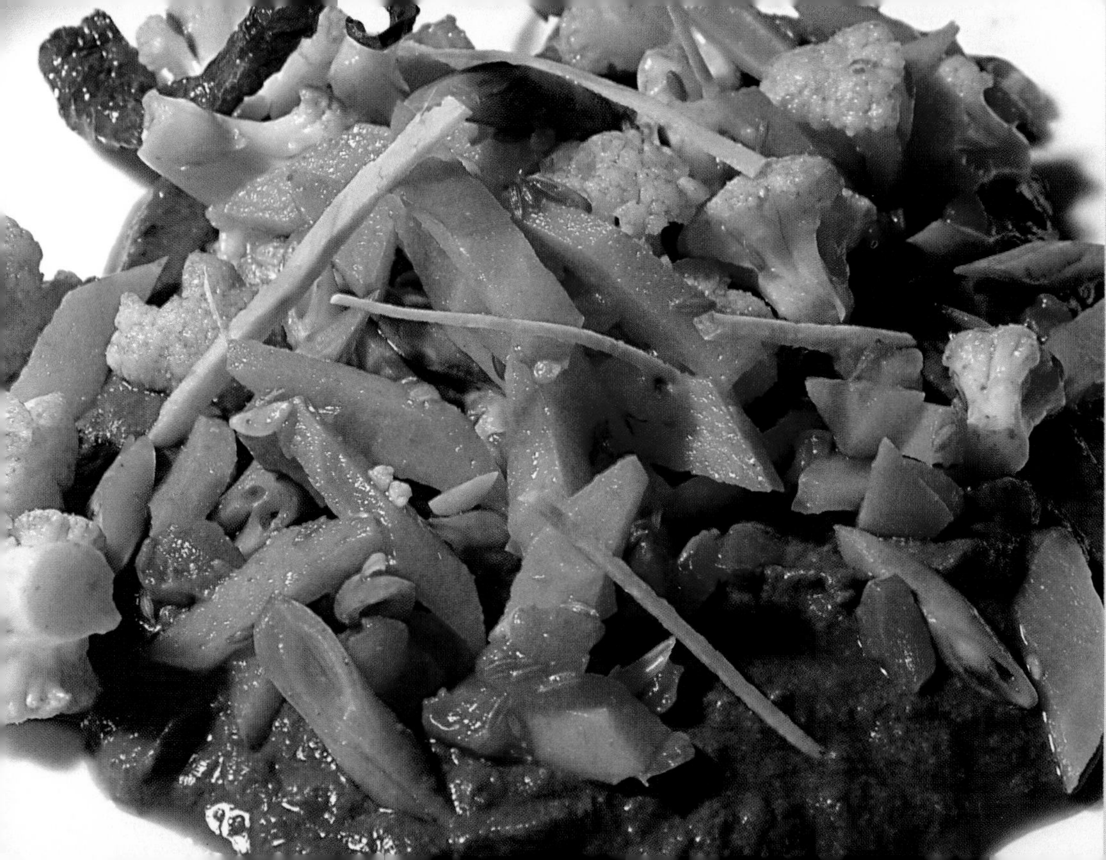

Palak Bahar

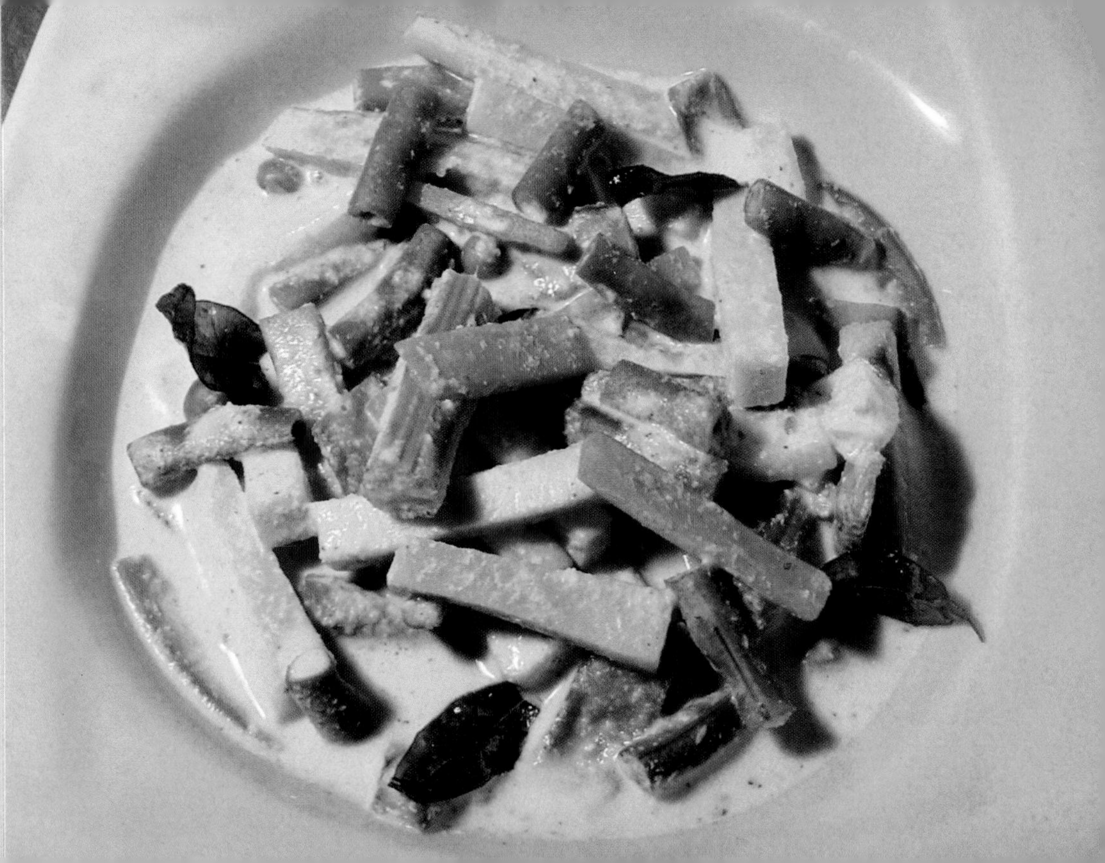

AVIYAL

INGREDIENTS

Carrot .... 1 medium sized
White pumpkin .... 200 gms
Raw banana .... 1 medium sized
Yam .... 100 gms
French beans 6-8
Broad beans 6-8
Drumstick 1
Green peas (shelled) .... ¼ cup
Curry leaves 10-12

Salt .... to taste
Yogurt .... 1½ cups
Coconut oil .... 2 tbsps
Paste
Coconut (scraped) .... ½ cup
Green chillies 4
Cumin seeds .... 1½ tsps
Rice .... 1 tbsp

METHOD OF PREPARATION

1   Peel, wash carrot, white pumpkin, raw banana and yam. String,
    wash French beans and broad beans. Cut these vegetables into finger
    sized batons measuring not more than two inches in length. Wash
    and cut drumstick into finger sized batons. Wash and drain green
    peas. Wash and pat dry curry leaves.

2 Boil yam separately in salted water. Drain and reserve.
3 To make paste, remove stems and wash green chillies. Grind coconut, green chillies, cumin seeds and rice to a fine paste. Whisk in yogurt and keep aside.
4 Boil carrot, white pumpkin, raw banana, French beans, broad beans, drumstick and peas and curry leaves in one and half cups of salted water. When vegetables are almost done, add yogurt mixture and stir thoroughly.
5 Bring to a simmering point and remove from heat. Lace with coconut oil and serve.

SICILIAN PASTA DON CAMILLO

INGREDIENTS

Spaghetti	200 gms	Fresh basil	a few leaves
Egg plant	1 medium sized	Sun dried tomatoes	50 gms
Olive oil	1 tbsp	Salt	to taste
Tomatoes	2 medium sized	Pepper (freshly crushed)	to taste
Garlic	4 cloves		

METHOD OF PREPARATION

1. Wash and cut egg plant into one inch cubes. Brush with olive oil and bake in a preheated oven for fifteen minutes at 200°C.
2. Wash and cut tomatoes into small dices. Peel, wash and chop garlic. Wash and tear basil leaves into small pieces. Reserve a few for garnish.
3. Clean and wash sundried tomatoes and soak them in hot water for ten to fifteen minutes. Chop them roughly.

4   Boil sufficient water in a large pan and add spaghetti and cook till almost done. Strain and refresh in cold running water and keep it aside.

5   Heat olive oil in a pan, sauté garlic and add tomatoes. Stir-fry for three to four minutes.

6   Add egg plant and stir-fry. Add spaghetti, salt, freshly crushed pepper and basil leaves. Cook on medium heat for a couple of minutes, stirring continuously.

7   Just before serving, add sundried tomatoes and toss.

8   Serve hot garnished with remaining basil leaves.

CARROT AND ONION FLORENTINE

INGREDIENTS

Carrots	3-4 medium sized	Oil	1 tsp
Onions	2 medium sized	Salt	to taste
Fresh spinach	2-3 medium bunches	White pepper powder	to taste
Broad beans (papdi)	100 gms	Skimmed milk	2 cups
Garlic	6-7 cloves	Mixed herbs (dried)	¼ tsp
Cornstarch	2 tbsps	Fresh brown bread crumbs	¼ cup

METHOD OF PREPARATION

1   Wash, peel and cut carrots into one and half centimeter sized cubes. Peel, wash and thinly slice onions. Clean, trim and thoroughly wash spinach in running water. Drain and finely chop. String, wash and cut broad beans into one and a half centimeter sized pieces. Peel, wash and lightly crush garlic. Dissolve cornstarch in a quarter cup of water.

2. Heat oil in a non-stick pan, add half the quantity of crushed garlic, stir briefly and add spinach. Sauté for four to five minutes over high heat, stirring occasionally or till the spinach is cooked completely. Add salt and white pepper to taste, stir well and remove from heat.

3 Heat skimmed milk in a saucepan and bring to a boil.

4 Add carrots, broad beans, onions and remaining garlic. Cover and simmer for three to four minutes, stirring frequently. Adjust salt and white pepper powder.

5 Gradually add blended cornstarch, stirring continuously, till it thickens to a fairly thick sauce consistency. Sprinkle mixed herbs, stir well and remove from heat. Keep warm.

6 Preheat oven to 180° C.

7 Take an ovenproof glass or a ceramic dish and layer the cooked spinach. Pour the cooked vegetables along with the sauce over the spinach and level it with a spatula.

8 Sprinkle fresh brown breadcrumbs on top of the vegetables and bake in a preheated oven at 180° C for ten minutes.

MASHORBA MUSHROOM

INGREDIENTS

Fresh button mushrooms 20-24	Melon seeds .... 1 tbsp
Onions .... 2 medium sized	Yogurt .... 2 tbsps
Ginger .... 2 one-inch pieces	Oil .... 4 tbsps
Garlic .... 4-6 cloves	Red chilli powder .... 1 tsp
Fresh coriander leaves	Coriander powder .... 1 tsp
.... ¼ medium bunch	Cumin powder .... ½ tsp
Tomatoes .... 2 medium sized	Salt .... to taste
Cashewnuts 10-12	*Garam masala* powder .... ½ tsp
Poppy seeds (*khus khus*) ... 1 tbsp	

METHOD OF PREPARATION

1   Clean, wash, pat dry and quarter mushrooms. Peel, wash and finely chop onions. Peel, wash ginger and garlic and grind to a fine paste. Clean, wash and finely chop fresh coriander leaves.

2 Wash, roughly chop and puree tomatoes in a blender. Soak cashewnuts, poppy seeds and melon seeds in one cup of hot water for ten minutes. Drain and grind to a fine paste. Whisk yogurt and keep aside.

3 Heat oil in a pan. Add onions and sauté for two to three minutes or until light brown in colour. Add ginger-garlic paste and stir-fry briefly.

4 Add red chilli powder, coriander powder, cumin powder and salt. Stir well and add prepared tomato puree. Cook on medium heat, stirring continuously, for two minutes or till oil separates. Add mushrooms and sauté for two minutes on high heat.

5 Dilute cashewnut-poppy-melon seeds paste in one and a half cups of water and add to mushroom mixture. Bring to a boil, reduce heat and simmer for five minutes or till mushrooms are cooked.

6 Sprinkle *garam masala* powder and chopped coriander leaves and serve hot.

MIDDLE EASTERN VEGETABLE STEW

INGREDIENTS

Capsicum .... 1 medium sized
Zucchinis .... 2 medium sized
Celery .... 1 stalk
Spinach .... ½ medium bunch
Carrots .... 2 medium sized
Potatoes .... 2 medium sized
Chickpeas .... ½ cup
Ginger .... 1 inch piece

Fresh mint leaves ...... a few sprigs
Vegetable stock .... 3 cups
Cloves 3-4
Peppercorns 8-10
Cumin powder .... 1 tsp
Red chilli powder .... a pinch
Salt .... to taste
Pepper powder .... ½ tsp

METHOD OF PREPARATION

1   Wash, halve and deseed capsicum. Wash zucchini. Trim and wash celery. Cut all into one inch sized pieces.

2   Clean, trim and wash spinach under running water and chop.

3　Peel, wash and cut carrots and potatoes into one inch-sized pieces.

4　Wash and soak chickpeas in sufficient water overnight. Pressure cook till done and keep aside.

5　Peel, wash and slice ginger. Clean, wash and chop mint leaves.

6　Heat vegetable stock in a saucepan and bring to a boil.

7　Tie ginger slices, cloves and peppercorns in a muslin cloth and add it to the boiling stock.

8　Add potatoes, boiled chickpeas, carrots, celery, cumin powder and red chilli powder. Mix well and cook on medium heat till it begins to boil.

9　Cover and simmer on low heat till all the vegetables are cooked and tender. Add the capsicum, zucchini, spinach and cook for two minutes. Remove bundle of ginger, cloves and peppercorns.

10　Season with salt and pepper powder and garnish with chopped mint leaves. Serve hot.

PHOOL GOBHI
SAMBHARI

INGREDIENTS

Cauliflower .... 1 medium sized
Onions .... 3 medium sized
Fresh coriander leaves ... a few sprigs
Tamarind .... one lemon sized ball
Coconut (scraped) .... ¾ cup
Oil .... 4 tbsps
Cumin seeds .... ½ tsp
Asafoetida .... ¼ tsp

Turmeric powder .... ½ tsp
Red chilli powder .... 1 tsp
Salt .... to taste
Sugar .... ½ tsp
Pathare Prabhu masala .... 1½ tsps
Cashewnuts 12-15
Gram flour *(besan)* .... ¼ cup

METHOD OF PREPARATION

1 Wash and cut cauliflower into small florets. Peel, wash and finely chop onions. Clean, wash and chop coriander leaves.
2 Soak tamarind in one cup of warm water for half an hour, remove the pulp, strain and keep aside.

3   Reserve one tablespoon of scraped coconut for garnishing. Soak the remaining scraped coconut in one and half cups of warm water. Grind and extract milk.

4   Heat oil in a pan, add cumin seeds and when they start to change colour, add asafoetida and onions. Sauté till onions turn translucent.

5   Add turmeric powder, red chilli powder, salt, sugar, *Pathare Prabhu masala,* cashewnuts and cauliflower florets. Mix well.

6   Add one cup of water and bring it to a boil. Reduce heat, cover and simmer for six to eight minutes.

7   Dissolve *besan* in half the quantity of coconut milk. Mix it well to ensure that there are no lumps and add this to the cauliflower mixture.

8   Increase heat and bring to a boil. Continue to cook on medium heat till cauliflower is cooked, stirring occasionally. Stir in the remaining coconut milk.

9   Serve hot, garnished with fresh coriander leaves and scraped coconut.

METHI MATAR MAKAI

INGREDIENTS

Fresh fenugreek leaves *(methi)* .. .. 1 large bunch
Green peas (shelled) .... 1 cup
Onions .... 2 medium sized
Ginger .... 1 inch piece
Garlic .... 5-6 cloves
Green chillies 3
Fresh coriander leaves ... a few sprigs
Fresh corn kernels .... 1 cup

Lemon juice .... 1 tbsp
Yogurt .... ½ cup
Turmeric powder .... a pinch
Red chilli powder .... 1 tsp
Oil .... 2 tbsps
Cumin seeds .... 1 tsp
Khoya/mawa (grated) .... ½ cup
Salt .... to taste
Fresh cream .... 1 cup

METHOD OF PREPARATION

1 Clean *methi* leaves, wash thoroughly and chop. Add one teaspoon of salt and set aside for half an hour. Squeeze dry and wash again. Wash and boil green peas.

2   Peel, wash onions and grate them. Peel and wash ginger and garlic and grind to a paste. Remove stems, wash and chop green chillies. Clean, wash and chop coriander leaves.

3   Boil corn in two cups of water and lemon juice till soft. Drain and keep aside. Whisk yogurt with turmeric and red chilli powders.

4   Heat oil in a pan. Add cumin seeds. When they start to crackle, add grated onion and cook till brown, stirring continuously. Add ginger-garlic paste and continue to cook. Add *methi* and green chillies. Cook till all the moisture dries up.

5   Add yogurt mixture and cook till oil separates. Add corn and green peas. Add *khoya* and one cup of water. Add salt to taste. Cook for ten minutes.

6   Stir in fresh cream and mix well. Simmer for five minutes. Serve hot.

KADAI VEGETABLES

INGREDIENTS

French beans 10-12
Carrots .... 2 medium sized
Capsicums.......... 2 medium sized
Cauliflower ...... ¼ medium sized
Tomatoes .... 3 large sized
Onions................ 2 medium sized
Green peas (shelled) .... ¼ cup
Red chillies whole.................. 4-5
Coriander seeds................ 1 tbsp
Cumin seeds .... 1 tsp

Garlic .... 12-15 cloves
Ginger .... 2 one inch pieces
Green chillies 3-4
Fresh coriander leaves ... a few sprigs
Oil .... 4 tbsps
Turmeric powder .... ½ tsp
Coriander powder .... 1 tbsp
Red chilli powder .... 1 tsp
Salt .... to taste
Garam masala powder .... 1 tsp

METHOD OF PREPARATION

1 String and wash French beans. Peel and wash carrots. Wash, halve
   and deseed capsicums. Cut all the vegetables into one-fourth inch
   cubes. Separate cauliflower into small florets and wash. Wash

tomatoes and chop them roughly. Peel, wash and slice onions. Wash and drain green peas. Remove stems and break red chillies into two.

2   Grind coarsely three of the red chillies with coriander and cumin seeds. Peel and wash garlic and ginger. Remove stems and wash green chillies. Clean, wash and chop coriander leaves.

3   Grind garlic, green chillies and half of the ginger to a paste. Make julienne of the rest of the ginger.

4   Heat oil in a pan. Add the coarsely ground *masala*. Add sliced onions and sauté till golden brown.

5   Add ginger-garlic-green chilli paste and sauté for one minute. Add the vegetables except capsicums and stir. Cook covered on low heat till carrots are almost done. Sprinkle a little water if necessary.

6   Add turmeric powder, coriander powder and red chilli powder. Stir continuously. Add tomatoes, salt and half a cup of water and cook till the vegetables are cooked and water dries up.

7   Add capsicums and salt. Cook for four to five minutes on low heat. Sprinkle *garam masala* powder.

8   Serve hot, garnished with ginger julienne and chopped coriander leaves.

Kadai Vegetables

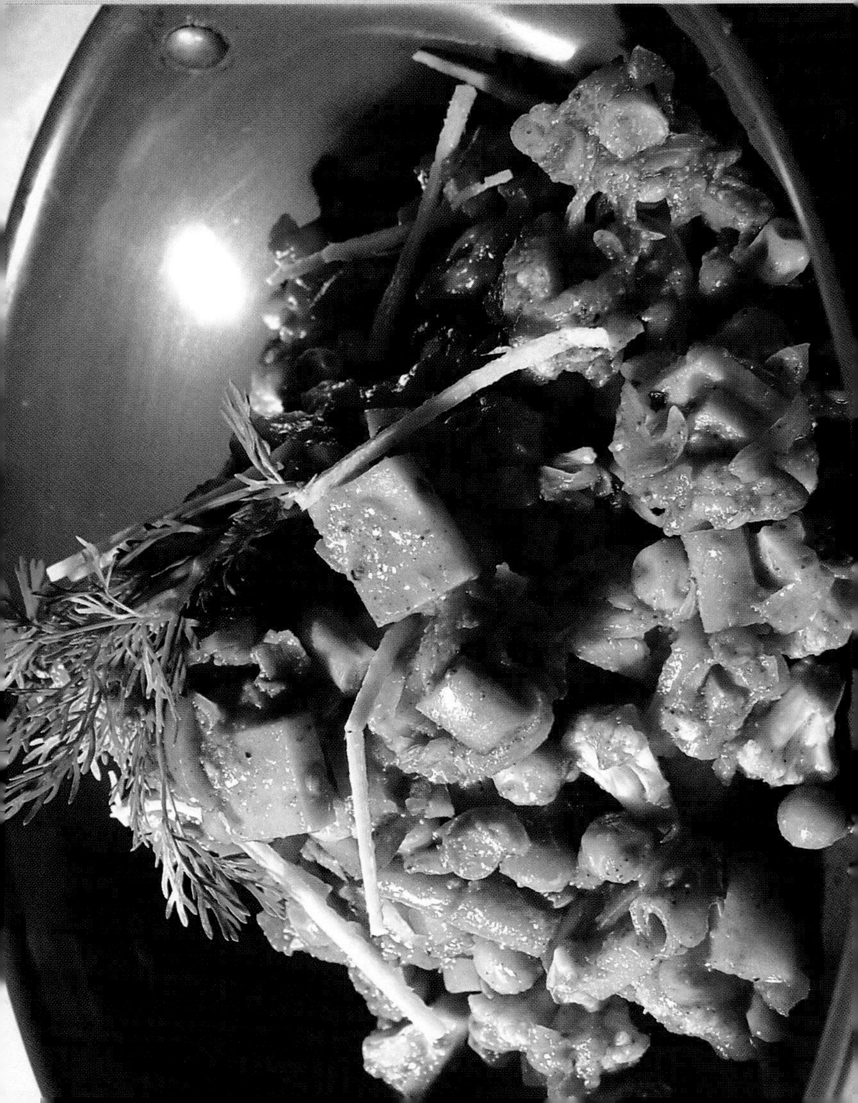

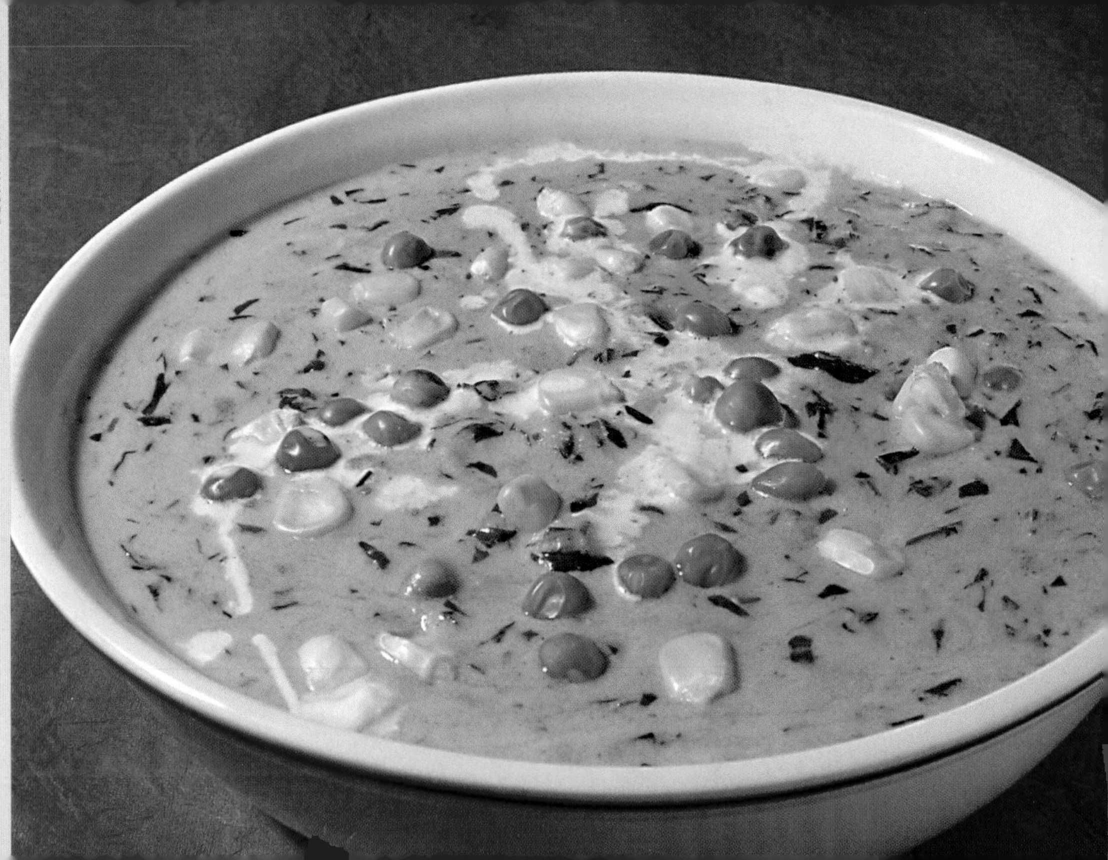

Methi Matar Makai

Dum Ki Arbi

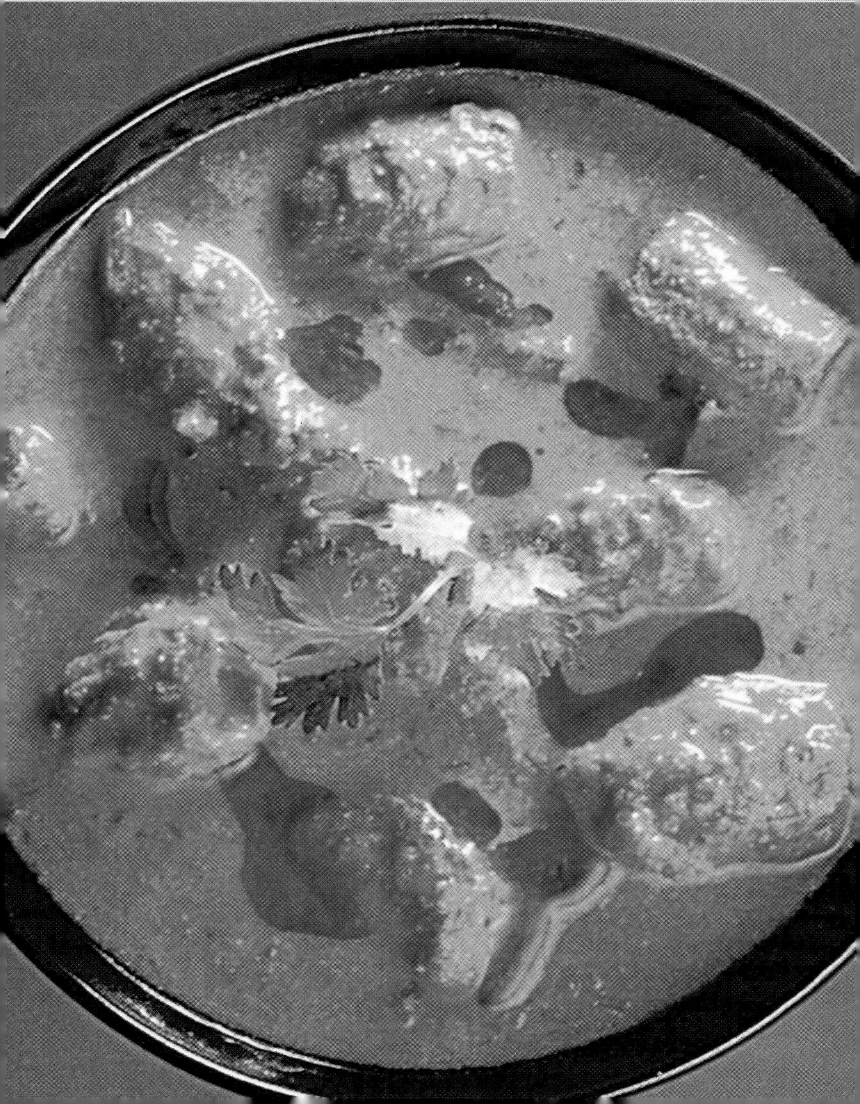

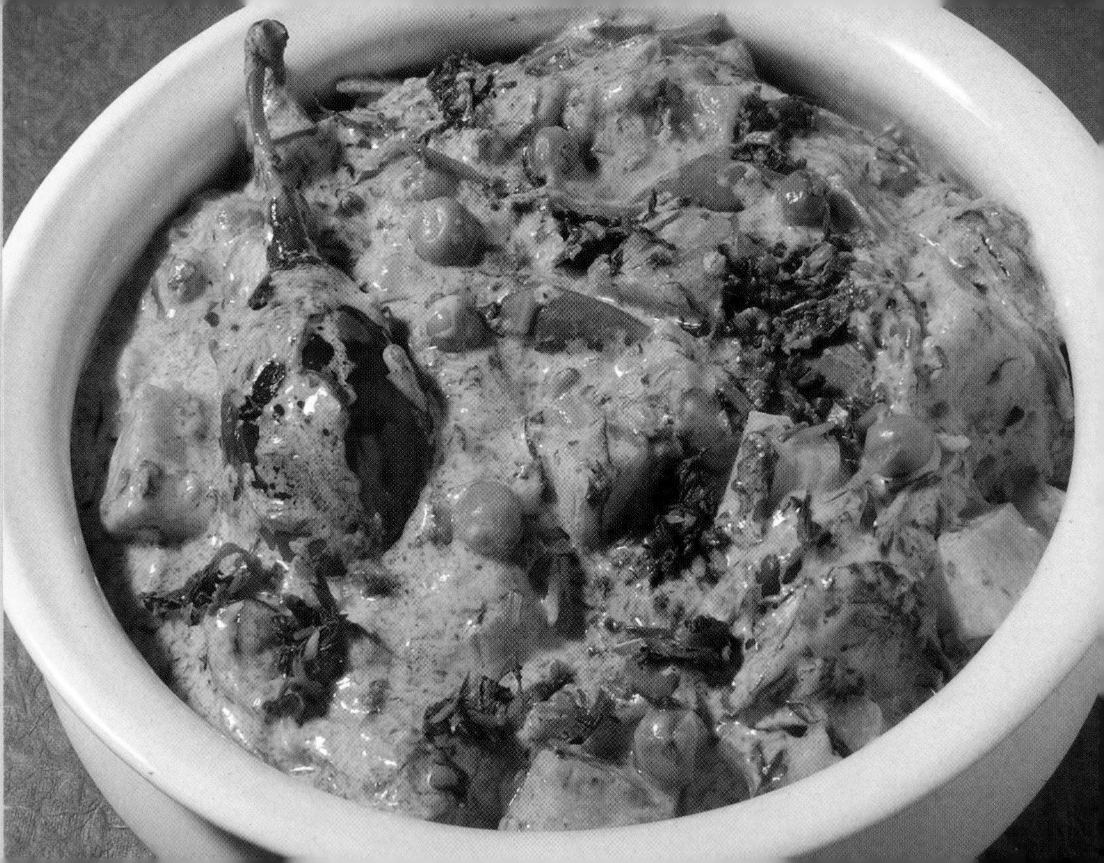

Diwani Handi

DIWANI HANDI

INGREDIENTS

Potatoes	3 medium sized	Fresh fenugreek leaves	½ bunch
Carrots	3 medium sized	Fresh coriander leaves	a few sprigs
French beans	10-12	Green chillies	2-3
Broad beans (*sem ki phalli*)	10-12	Oil	3 tbsps
Brinjals	4-6 small sized	Red chilli powder	1 tsp
Onions	2 medium sized	Turmeric powder	½ tsp
Ginger	1½ inch piece	Salt	to taste
Garlic	10 cloves	Yogurt	2 tbsps
Green peas (shelled)	½ cup	*Garam masala*	½ tsp

METHOD OF PREPARATION

1   Peel, wash and cut potatoes and carrots into half inch sized cubes. String, wash and cut French beans and broad beans diagonally. Wash and slit brinjals into two. Peel, wash and thinly slice onions. Peel,

wash and grind ginger and garlic to a fine paste. Wash and drain green peas.

2   Clean, wash and chop fresh fenugreek leaves and coriander leaves. Remove stems, deseed and chop green chillies.

3   Heat oil in a *handi*, add onions and sauté till light brown. Add green chillies, ginger-garlic paste and sauté for a minute. Add red chilli powder, turmeric powder, salt and mix.

4   Add yogurt and stir-fry for two to three minutes.

5   Add all the vegetables and simmer, covered, till the vegetables are cooked.

6   Add fenugreek leaves, coriander leaves and *garam masala*, stir and cook for three to four minutes.

7   Serve hot with *Hyderabadi parantha* or any other Indian bread of your choice.

DUM KI ARBI

INGREDIENTS

Colocassia *(arbi)* .... 700 gms	Cumin powder .... 1 tsp
Oil .... 4 tbsps + to deep fry	Turmeric powder .... ½ tsp
Onions .... 3 medium sized	Green cardamoms 4-6
Ginger .... 1½ inch piece	Coriander powder .... 1 tsp
Garlic .... 10 cloves	Nutmeg (grated) .... ¼ tsp
Poppy seeds *(khus khus)* .. 3 tbsps	*Garam masala* powder .... ½ tsp
Yogurt .... 2 cups	Salt .... to taste
Red chilli powder .... ½ tsp	Fresh cream .... ¼ cup

METHOD OF PREPARATION

1   Wash, peel and cut *arbi* into one inch sized pieces. Heat sufficient oil in a *kadai* and deep fry *arbi* till crisp and golden brown. Drain onto an absorbent paper and keep aside.

2   Peel, wash onions and cut into halves. Add two cups of water and boil till soft. Drain off excess water, cool and grind to a smooth paste. Peel, wash and grind ginger and garlic to a fine paste.

3   Dry roast poppy seeds and soak in water for half an hour. Grind to a smooth paste. Whisk yogurt along with red chilli powder, cumin powder and turmeric powder.

4   Heat four tablespoons of oil in a pan. Add green cardamoms. When they start to change colour slightly, add boiled onion paste. Sauté till light golden brown. Add ginger-garlic paste and coriander powder. Mix well. Stir in poppy seeds paste and cook for a minute.

5   Add whisked yogurt, bring it to a boil. Add fried *arbi*, grated nutmeg, *garam masala* powder and salt.

6   Cover pan with a tight fitting lid and simmer for thirty minutes. Alternatively, cover pan with aluminum foil or seal the lid with wheat flour dough (*atta*), so that the aroma is contained in the pan and does not escape.

7   Just before serving open the lid and stir in fresh cream.

METHI TOMATO PANEER

INGREDIENTS

Low-fat *paneer* .... 200 gms
Fresh fenugreek leaves *(methi)* ...
.... 1 medium bunch
Tomatoes .... 4 medium sized
Ginger .... 1 inch piece
Garlic .... 6 cloves
Onions .... 2 medium sized

Green chillies 2-3
Oil .... 1 tbsp
Kashmiri red chilli powder ... 1 tsp
Coriander powder .... 1 tbsp
Salt .... to taste
Dried mango powder *(amchur)* ..
.... 1 tsp

METHOD OF PREPARATION

1   Cut *paneer* into half inch sized cubes.
2   Clean, wash and chop fresh *methi* leaves.
3   Wash and finely chop tomatoes. Peel and wash ginger, garlic and
    onions. Chop onions finely.

4   Remove stems, wash green chillies and grind to a paste with ginger and garlic.

5   Heat oil in a non-stick pan, add onions and sauté for three to four minutes or till it just starts turning brown.

6   Add ginger-garlic-green chili paste, stir-fry briefly and add Kashmiri red chilli powder, coriander powder and salt to taste. Mix well.

7   Immediately add *methi* leaves and cook on medium heat, stirring frequently for six to eight minutes, stirring continuously or till *methi* leaves are completely cooked and dry.

8   Add tomatoes, stir and cook over high heat for two to three minutes. Add half a cup of water, cover and simmer for three to four minutes.

9   Add *paneer*, sprinkle dried mango powder and mix well. Heat thoroughly and serve immediately.

KACHA KOLAR DALNA

INGREDIENTS

Raw bananas ...... 4 medium sized
Gram flour *(besan)* .... 2 tbsps
Ginger .... 2 inch piece
Garlic .... 6-8 cloves
Fresh coriander leaves ....
.... ¼ small bunch
Onion .... 1 large sized
Tomato .... 1 medium sized

Red chilli powder .... 1 tsp
Salt .... to taste
Oil .... 1 tbsp + to deep fry
Bay leaf 1
Turmeric powder .... ½ tsp
Salt .... to taste
Garam masala powder .... ½ tsp

METHOD OF PREPARATION

1   Wash, boil and cool raw bananas. Peel and mash thoroughly.
2   Peel, wash ginger and garlic and grind to a fine paste. Clean, wash
    and finely chop coriander leaves. Peel, wash and grate onion. Wash
    and finely chop tomato.

3 Mix mashed banana, coriander leaves, gram flour, one teaspoon of ginger-garlic paste, half a teaspoon of red chilli powder and salt to taste. Knead to a dough and divide into ten to twelve equal portions. Shape them into round *koftas*.

4 Heat sufficient oil in a *kadai* and deep fry *koftas* on medium heat till golden brown. Drain onto an absorbent kitchen towel.

5 Heat one tablespoon of oil in a pan. Add bay leaf and onion. Sauté till onion turns translucent and add remaining ginger-garlic paste and stir-fry briefly.

6 Add red chilli powder, turmeric powder, tomato and cook on low heat, stirring continuously, till oil separates.

7 Add two cups of water and salt to taste and bring the gravy to a boil. Reduce heat and add fried *koftas*. Simmer for five minutes. Stir in *garam masala* powder and serve hot.

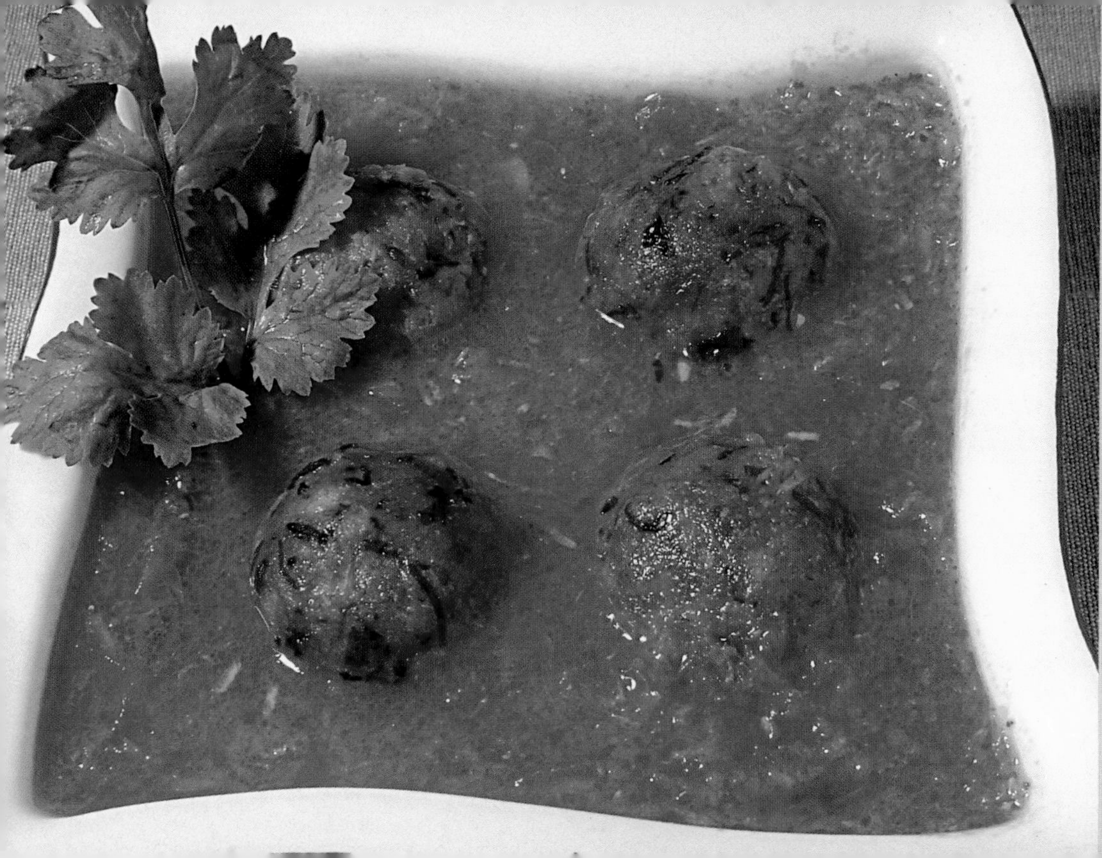

Kacha Kolar Dalna

OONDHIYU

INGREDIENTS

Sweet potato ..... 1 medium sized
Yam (*kand*) .... ½ medium sized
Small *papdi* beans .... 100 gms
Tuvar dana .... 1/3 cup
Ginger .... ½ inch piece
Garlic .... 3-4 cloves
Small brinjals 2-3
Baby potatoes 4
Oil.............................. 2 tbsps
Carom seeds (*ajwain*) .... 1 tsp
Asafoetida...................... a pinch
Soda bicarbonate............ a pinch
Coriander powder.............. ½ tsp
Garam masala powder .... a pinch
Salt .... to taste
For the green masala stuffing ....
Green peas (shelled)............¼ cup
Coconut (scraped) .... ¼ cup
Fresh coriander leaves ... a few sprigs

Green garlic .... 4-5 stalks
Green chillies 3-4
Garlic 2-3
Sesame seeds .... ½ tbsp
Garam masala powder .... ½ tsp
Coriander powder .... 1 tsp
Turmeric powder .... a pinch
Soda bicarbonate.. a small pinch
Lemon juice .... ½ tbsp
Salt .... to taste
For the muthiya
Fenugreek leaves ..... ¼ small bunch
Gram flour (*besan*) ....¼ cup
Wholewheat flour (coarse)... ½ cup
Turmeric powder .... ½ tsp
Oil .... 2 tbsps + to deep fry
Coriander-cumin powder ..... ½ tbsp
Salt .... to taste

METHOD OF PREPARATION

1   To make the *muthiyas* clean, wash and chop *methi*. Mix with *besan*, *atta*, turmeric powder, two tablespoons of oil, cumin-coriander powder and salt. Mix well. Knead into a stiff dough using water only if needed. Divide into ten equal portions and shape into one-inch long and half-inch thick rolls. Heat sufficient oil in a *kadai* and deep fry *muthiya* in hot oil till golden brown. Drain onto an absorbent paper and keep aside.

2   Peel, wash and cut yam and sweet potato into cubes. In the same oil deep fry the yam and sweet potato till golden brown. Remove onto an absorbent paper and keep aside. Peel and wash potatoes. String *papdi*, split into two and wash. Wash *tuvar dana*. Peel, wash and grind together ginger and garlic.

3   For stuffing, wash and drain peas. Clean, wash and chop coriander leaves and green garlic. Remove stems, wash and finely chop green chillies. Peel, wash and crush garlic. In a bowl mix all the ingredients of the green *masala* stuffing and adjust seasoning. Keep a little of coriander leaves, coconut and green garlic aside for garnishing.

4   Wash and slit brinjals. Stuff them with this *masala* and mix one-

fourth cup of the green *masala* with the potatoes and keep aside. Keep aside the remaining *masala* for further use.

5   Take a deep thick bottomed *degchi*. Heat oil, add carom seeds and allow to splutter. Add asafoetida.

6   Add the *papdi* beans, *tuvar dana* and stir well and fry for two minutes.

7   Add ginger-garlic paste. Stir once. Add soda bicarbonate, coriander powder, *garam masala* powder salt and remaining green *masala*. Stir once or twice. Add half a cup of water, mix well and as it starts to boil, lower heat and spread over this stuffed brinjals and stuffed potatoes. Cover with a lid and pour some water on the lid. Cook on low heat.

8   Check every few minutes, tossing occasionally, taking care to keep the stuffed vegetables on the top. Place the fried yam and sweet potatoes when *papdi* is half done.

9   Cover and continue to cook till nearly done. Best is to check the seed of the *papdi* bean or a brinjal for doneness. Add the fried *muthiyas* and cover and allow to simmer on low heat till the *muthiyas* double in size.

10 Serve hot, garnished with chopped coriander, chopped fresh green garlic and scraped coconut.

TINDLI MOONGFALI

INGREDIENTS

Peanuts (shelled)	1 cup	Mustard seeds	1 tsp
Tindli	500 gms	Red chilli powder	1 tsp
Curry leaves	8-10	Coriander powder	2 tsps
Ginger	1 inch piece	Turmeric powder	½ tsp
Garlic	6-7 cloves	Cumin powder	½ tsp
Green chillies	1-2	Salt	to taste
Oil	2 tbsps		

METHOD OF PREPARATION

1 Wash and cut *tindli* into thin slices. Leave aside. Wash and pat dry curry leaves. Peel, wash and grind ginger and garlic to a paste. Remove stems, wash and finely chop green chillies.

2 Heat oil, add mustard seeds and curry leaves. As mustard seeds start crackling, add ginger-garlic paste and green chillies. Cook for a minute, stirring well.

3 Add shelled peanuts and cook till they are slightly browned.

4 Add *tindli* and continue stir-frying till *tindli* is half done.

5 Add red chilli powder, coriander powder, turmeric powder, cumin powder and salt. Mix thoroughly and cook on low heat till cooked and dry. Serve hot.

RATATOUILLE

INGREDIENTS

Long egg plants (brinjal) .... 2 medium sized
Zucchini .... 2 medium sized
Salt .... to taste
Onions .... 2 medium sized
Garlic .... 4 cloves
Tomatoes .... 3 medium sized

Capsicum .... 2 medium sized
Fresh basil leaves .... a few
Olive oil .... 1 tbsp
Tomato puree .... 4 tbsps
White pepper powder .... to taste
Coriander powder .... ¼ tsp
Cinnamon powder .... a pinch

METHOD OF PREPARATION

1   Wash and halve egg plants and zucchini lengthways. Cut them further into thick slices.

2   Place egg plants in a colander and sprinkle with salt. Top with a weighted plate and leave to degorge for one hour.

3   Peel, wash and slice onions into rings. Peel, wash and chop garlic.

4   Wash and remove eyes of tomatoes, make a cross slit on the bottom side and immerse in boiling water for half a minute. Drain, peel,

deseed and chop them roughly.

5   Wash, halve, deseed and cut capsicum into thin strips. Wash and shred fresh basil leaves.

6   Heat olive oil in a non-stick pan and cook onions over low heat till translucent. Stir in tomato puree and cook on medium heat for three to four minutes, stirring occasionally. Rinse egg plants and drain well. Add them to the cooking pan along with zucchini.

7   Add garlic and capsicum and simmer for about five minutes.

8   Add tomatoes, white pepper powder, coriander powder, cinnamon powder, shredded basil, salt and pepper. Stir once or twice and cook over medium heat for about ten minutes, stirring frequently.

9   Adjust seasoning and serve hot.

ORANGE
BROCCOLI

INGREDIENTS

Broccoli	2 medium sized	Light soy sauce	1 tbsp
Carrots	2 medium sized	Honey	1 tsp
Ginger	1 inch piece	Oil	2 tbsps
Garlic	4-6 cloves	Salt	to taste
Oranges	2 large sized	Pepper powder	to taste
Cornstarch	2 tbsps		

METHOD OF PREPARATION

1 Wash broccoli well and separate into small florets. Peel stem and slice thinly. Wash, peel and thinly slice carrots.
2 Peel, wash and thinly slice ginger and garlic.
3 Squeeze the juice of oranges and mix with cornstarch, soy sauce, honey and half a cup of water. Reserve a little orange peel. Cut into

thin strips and keep in cold water.

4   Heat oil in a pan. Add broccoli stems and carrots and stir-fry for about two minutes.

5   Add ginger, garlic and broccoli florets, stir-fry for another two minutes. Sprinkle a little water and cook for two to three minutes.

6   Stir in orange juice mixture, cook on high heat for about a minute, stirring continuously. Do not overcook. Add salt and pepper.

7   Remove orange rind from cold water and stir into the pan before serving.

SHANGHAI STIR FRIED VEGETABLES

INGREDIENTS

Carrots .... 1 medium sized
Capsicum .... 1 medium sized
Onion .... 1 medium sized
Cauliflower .... ¼ small sized
Baby corns 6-8
Chinese cabbage ... ½ medium sized
Fresh button mushrooms 8-10
Spring onions 2

Garlic .... 6-8 cloves
Water chestnuts (optional) .. 3-4
Cornstarch .... 1 tbsp
Oil .... 1 tsp
Light soy sauce .... 1 tbsp
Salt .... to taste
White pepper powder .... ¼ tsp

METHOD OF PREPARATION

1 Peel carrots, wash and cut into two lengthwise and thinly slice.
2 Wash capsicum, halve, deseed and cut into one inch sized pieces.
3 Peel, wash and cut onion into quarters and separate onion segments.
4 Wash and separate cauliflowers into small sized florets and slice them into two through the stem.

5   Wash, trim and slice baby corns into three to four pieces diagonally. Separate Chinese cabbage leaves and wash thoroughly under running water. Drain well and cut into one inch sized pieces.

6   Wash mushrooms thoroughly and cut them into quarters. Peel, wash and slice spring onion along with some greens. Peel, wash garlic and crush lightly. Peel, wash and slice water chestnuts.

7   Dissolve cornstarch in half a cup of water. Keep aside.

8   Heat oil in a non-stick wok, add garlic, stir and add carrots, cauliflower, baby corns and mushrooms. Toss well and sprinkle a little water on vegetables. Cook on high heat, stirring frequently, for two to three minutes.

9   Add onion segments, capsicum, water chestnuts and Chinese cabbage. Stir-fry on high heat again for two minutes, stirring frequently. Add soy sauce and salt and white pepper powder to taste. Toss well.

10 Mix blended cornstarch and add to the vegetables, stirring continuously. Cook further for a minute. Serve immediately.

SAFFRON AND SPINACH CASSEROLE

INGREDIENTS

Pasta (macaroni) .... 1 cup
Oil.. 1 tbsp
Onion .... 1 large sized
Garlic .... 15 cloves
French beans 8-10
Zucchini .... 1 medium sized
Carrots .... 2 medium sized
Broccoli............. ½ medium sized
Spinach ....½ medium bunch
Butter .... 3 tbsps

Refined flour *(maida)* ..... 1 tbsp
Milk .... 1½ cups
Nutmeg (grated) .... a pinch
Cheese (grated) .... 1 cup
Salt .... to taste
Pepper powder .... ¼ tsp
Peppercorns (freshly crushed) ....
.... ¼ tsp
Saffron............. a generous pinch

METHOD OF PREPARATION

1   Heat four cups of water, bring it to boil, add one tablespoon of oil
    and pasta. Boil till it is nearly done. Do not overcook pasta. Drain
    and refresh under cold water.

2   Peel, wash and chop onion and garlic.
3   String and wash French beans. Wash zucchini and peel and wash carrots. Cut all these into diamond shapes. Wash and break broccoli into florets. Clean and trim spinach. Boil seven to eight cups of water and blanch French beans, zucchini, broccoli, spinach and carrots one by one. Puree blanched spinach.
4   Heat one tablespoon of butter and lightly sauté refined flour. Gradually add one cup milk and stir continuously so that no lumps remain. Add nutmeg, some cheese, salt and pepper powder. This is mornay sauce.
5   Heat another tablespoon of butter in a pan, add garlic and sauté till golden brown. Add onion and sauté till golden brown.
6   Add beans, broccoli, zucchini and salt and sauté well.
7   Add half of the mornay sauce, one fourth cup of milk and mix well.
8   Add spinach puree and half of the freshly crushed peppercorns and mix well.
9   Dissolve saffron in remaining one fourth cup of milk.
10 In another pan, heat remaining butter and sauté carrots. Add boiled pasta, remaining mornay sauce, saffron milk and mix well. Add salt. Cook for sometime and add remaining freshly crushed peppercorns.

11 Preheat oven to 225° C.
12 Pour green vegetable mixture into an oven proof dish.
13 Spread half of the grated cheese on the green vegetable mixture and then pour the carrots-pasta mixture over it. Again spread a layer of remaining grated cheese and bake for five to ten minutes in a preheated oven at 225° C till cheese melts and turns golden.

KOREAN PICKLED VEGETABLES

INGREDIENTS

Red radishes (round) .... 3-4 small sized
White radish ...... 1 medium sized
Fresh button mushrooms 10-15
Carrots .... 2 medium sized
Turnips .... 2 medium sized
Cauliflower .... ½ medium sized
Garlic .... 6-8 cloves
Green chillies 3-4

Spring onions 3
Ginger .... 1 inch piece
Soy sauce .... 1 tbsp
Pepper powder .... 1 tsp
Red chillies whole 2
Lemon leaves 2-3
Star anise 1-2
Salt .... to taste
White vinegar .... ¾ cup

METHOD OF PREPARATION

1 Wash, trim and quarter red radishes.

2 Peel, wash and cut white radish into one and a half inch long thin strips.

3 Clean, wash mushrooms well and cut into quarters.

4 Peel, wash and cut carrots and turnips into one and a half inch long thin strips.

5 Cut cauliflower into small florets, wash and soak in warm salted water for ten to fifteen minutes. Drain and keep aside.

6 Peel and wash garlic. Wash green chillies and keep them whole. Peel, wash and trim spring onions, discard the greens and reserve the onion whole.

7 Peel, wash and cut ginger into thin slices.

8 Heat two and a half cups of water with soy sauce, ginger, pepper powder, red chillies, lemon leaves, garlic, star anise and salt to taste. Bring to a boil, reduce heat and simmer for two to three minutes.

9 Add vinegar, the prepared vegetables including green chillies. Remove from heat immediately and stir well.

10 Pour into a glass or ceramic jar and cool. Cover jar with a muslin cloth and let vegetables pickle for two days at room

temperature, before using. Stir two to three times a day for uniform pickling.

11 Refrigerate and use a slotted spoon to remove the pickle as and when required. It has a shelf life of two to three weeks.

Korean Pickled Vegetables

Spinach and Saffron Casserole